Polytechnic Days
Texas Wesleyan's First Decade
1891-1901

By Risa Brown

Alliance Publishing LLC
Dallas, Texas

Texas Wesleyan University Decade by Decade Series

Polytechnic Days:
Texas Wesleyan's First Decade 1891-1901

Best Equipped and Most Loved:
Texas Wesleyan's Second Decade 1901-1911

Copyright © 2020 Alliance Publishing LLC

ISBN: 978-1-7345702-0-5
Library of Congress Control Number: 2020901901

Alliance Publishing, LLC
Dallas, Texas

All rights reserved. No part of this book may be reproduced, transmitted, or stored in any form or by any means, graphic, electronic, or mechanical, including photocopying, taping, and recording, without prior written permission from the publisher.

Printed in the United States of America.

Cover Photo: Polytechnic Class of 1900.
Courtesy of Ann Ahlbrand Robinson, M.Ed.

TABLE OF CONTENTS

INTRODUCTION		5
One	THE PRESIDENT AND THE GHOST	9
Two	ENTRANCE REQUIREMENTS	13
Three	HOW MUCH DID IT COST?	17
Four	PROFILE: C. L. BROWNING	19
Five	FACULTY	21
Six	PROFILE: LEE RIPPEY	23
Seven	PROFILE: EDWIN SPURLOCK	27
Eight	RULES FOR GIRLS	29
Nine	PROFILE: ROLAND BROOKS & WESSIE ADKISSON	33
Ten	THE HALL FAMILY	35
Eleven	THE TANDY FAMILY	41
Twelve	RELIGIOUS FERVOR	45
Thirteen	SCHOLARSHIPS	47
Fourteen	PROFILE: LIZZIE ADKISSON	49
Fifteen	PROFILE: INNIE KIDD	51
Sixteen	BOARD OF TRUSTEES	53
Seventeen	PHILOSOPHIANS AND ADKISSONIANS: THE LITERARY SOCIETIES	57

Eighteen	**THE SUSAN M. KEYS: WOMEN'S LITERARY SOCIETY**	63
Nineteen	**PROFILE: MARVIN COPPEDGE & ADA BROOKS**	67
Twenty	**EAST SIDE OF TOWN: POLYTECHNIC HEIGHTS**	69
Twenty-one	**PROFILE: NOBLE ADKISSON & ANNA KANOUSE**	75
Twenty-two	**TROUBLEMAKERS AND PRANKSTERS**	77
Twenty-three	**PROFILE: LEON SENSABAUGH**	81
Twenty-four	**PROFILE: GEORGE SENSABAUGH**	85
Twenty-five	**DEGREE PLANS**	87
Twenty-six	**PROFILE: ELLA RAY LEDGERWOOD**	93
Twenty-seven	**POLY SPORTS**	97
Twenty-eight	**PROFILE: FRED NEWSOM**	101
Twenty-nine	**PROFILE: SAM KANOUSE**	103
Thirty	**EVERYTHING THAT COULD GO WRONG AND DID**	107
Thirty-one	**PROFILE: ANTON LAPORTE THOMAS**	111
Thirty-two	**CLASS OF 1900**	113
CONCLUSION		117
ACKNOWLEDGEMENTS		121
ENDNOTES		122
BIBLIOGRAPHY		123
PHOTOGRAPHS		126

INTRODUCTION

In August 1890, the Methodist Episcopal Church South sent Reverend Milton Koger Little to evaluate a land donation. Bishop Joseph S. Key had been recently appointed to the North Texas conference and he had a vision: a great college that would teach classes in well, everything. Now that he was in Fort Worth, it was time to make his dream a reality. He sold the idea to the conference, and now Little was charged with making a choice on where they would build it. He had three properties to choose from and he liked the largest one, away from town, where they had room to expand.

Four miles outside of Fort Worth, the Hall brothers Arch and W. D., along with George Tandy, combined their land to offer a 50 acre tract. If the church wanted wide open space there was plenty, along with lots of prairie grass.

More than a hundred years later, Texas Wesleyan University is thriving and modern; Fort Worth is the 16th largest city in the U. S. and one of the fastest growing.

Before the college was even a thought in the bishop's head, the fort that gave Fort Worth its

Tandy Hills Natural Area
Courtesy of photographer Don Young.

name had long been abandoned by the Army. After the Civil War, the village surrounding the fort embraced being a stop on the cattle trails—a role which breathed life into the fledgling town. One side-effect of the cattle business was a rough Wild West character and a doozy of an entertainment district known as "Hell's Half Acre." For a while, Fort Worth was content with that.

Then the railroad changed everything.

Now business owners of all kinds were confident of their chances in Fort Worth. The city exploded and profit was easy. The new prosperous citizens had money and influence and, by golly, they wanted a civilized town. This roughshod bunch just wouldn't do.

Churches of all denominations began early in the town's development, but now congregations outgrew their buildings. People demanded law and order. If they were going to be a legitimate town, those cowboys could no longer rule the roost.

Stores offered stylish clothes. People built bigger, grander homes and had babies. The folks who wanted a wholesome town had socials of all kinds, parades, and a lake with a pavilion. Fort Worth resembled River City of the Music Man fame rather than Tombstone, Arizona. Its citizens wanted no more *trouble with a capital T*, as Harold Hill warned.

The way to combat this issue was education. Churches led the way by establishing colleges and private schools. One college, known as Fort Worth University, was established in 1881 by the Methodist Episcopal Church North. Later, thanks to the Disciples of Christ, TCU would move to Fort Worth and the Baptists introduced Southwest Baptist Theological Seminary.

The Southern branch of the Methodist Episcopal Church was new to the college scene when they started organizing Polytechnic College. Once the land was donated and divided into lots, the college could then sell the lots they were not going to use to raise valuable funds for buildings and faculty salaries. A town would soon spring up around the college with businesses and homes, even a mill.

What was Fort Worth like in 1890?

A rising star with a population just a touch over 25,000. With changes in cattle breeds and rail transport, cattle drives dwindled to a trickle. As neighborhood and subdivisions grew, lots were being cut into the prairie, electric streetcars were laying routes to outlying areas, and women were holding fundraisers for a public library.

Initially, children were educated by private tutors. The idea of public education was a hard sell; folks just didn't see the need. But the city fathers pressed on, and Fort Worth organized the first school board to establish public education.

Fires were common in a town with hastily built wooden houses and businesses and lighting still provided by oil lanterns. A fire brigade had been in existence since 1873 with dozens of volunteers and one horse drawn hook-and-ladder wagon. The five alarm system consisted of the

Bird's eye view of Fort Worth when Polytechnic opened its doors.
Courtesy, Library of Congress, Geography and Maps Division.

man nearest the fire shooting his six-shooter in the air and a seven-year-old running to the firehouse and ringing the bell as hard as he could.

It was time for an upgrade, especially after the disastrous events that would take place in the spring of 1891.

Fort Worth was proud of its latest landmark, the Texas Spring Palace. More than an exhibition hall, it was a symbol of the town's great optimism. Inspired by Canadian Ice Palaces and Iowa's Corn Palace, the Spring Palace was a place to show off all things Texan. Constructed only out of Texas resources, the palace was a cross between a castle and the Taj Mahal. It was described as "the most beautiful structure on earth" with pride and affection.

Only a year after it opened, a fancy dress ball was held with estimates of 7,000 in attendance. Unfortunately, the building caught fire, and within thirty minutes it burned to the ground. Surprisingly only one man was killed: a hero going in over and over to rescue people inside.

Polytechnic College's first school year followed right after this blow to the community, opening in September of 1891.

The Texas Spring Palace, 1890
*Courtesy, Jack White Photograph Collection, Special Collections,
The University of Texas at Arlington Libraries.*

ONE
THE PRESIDENT AND THE GHOST

Colleges don't spring up overnight and the Southern Methodist Episcopals knew it. Once the land was staked and claimed, a boom of activity began with the utmost optimism.

The new college was called Polytechnic (literally meaning *many arts*) because the founding fathers added science and, radical for the times, business degrees. Fort Worth was growing thanks to multiple industries, so business skills were thought to be especially advantageous. Other colleges focused on arts and the classics, so from its inception Polytechnic was forward thinking.

Earliest photograph of Polytechnic campus.
*Courtesy, Texas Wesleyan University Special Collections
(Maud Hunter Collection).*

Money was slow to come, so organizers had to be content with one brick building which would serve as administration central as well as classroom space. Add to that two wooden structures: a dormitory for men and the chapel. That was the extent of the new campus when students showed up for the 1891-92 school year.

The conference organizers also found a president. John W. Adkisson's experience as a headmaster at other Methodist colleges made him a good candidate to lead Polytechnic. Before he was even twenty, he earned his credentials as a pastor and worked in Missouri as a circuit riding preacher during the Civil War. According to his obituary, "His life and liberty were constantly in peril. His presiding elder and other preachers were shot down by the roadside, and he was urged by his friends to quit going to his appointments, but he expressed a determination rather to die than to desert his post of duty."

When he was hired by Central College in Sulphur Springs, family records say John brought his wife and children to Texas from Meridian, Mississippi, in a covered wagon over dirt roads, crossing the Mississippi River at Vicksburg. They brought what food and furniture they could carry. When he was appointed to Polytechnic, many of his children (somewhat grown, let's hope) were also hired as teachers.

Based on his early fortitude, John must have shown the strength it took to organize a new college, but he was also described as "kind and gentle and tender as a woman." He lived the saying 'never mistake a quiet man for a weak one.' Certainly he was willing to roll up his sleeves and teach when it was needed, in addition to being an administrator.

For the first year of classes, 1891-92, John and his wife Annie along with their children who still lived with them, took care of the female students who lived on campus. Annie appeared to be her husband's equal in work. In her obituary, she was called his "right hand," a manager of a boarding school in her own right. The young ladies of Polytechnic "felt that she was a mother indeed and they gave her unbounded love and confidence."[1]

She loved them so much that, when she was dying, she included them as loved ones during her final hours. "She called in her children and the young lady boarders and bid them all an affectionate farewell, urging them to meet her in heaven."

Annie was the first person buried in the new Polytechnic cemetery. Her funeral was held in the college chapel with the Rev. W. F. Lloyd presiding. Rev. Lloyd would soon become the president of Polytechnic.

A recession hit in 1893 and the local economy sank out of control. The optimism that once buoyed the college lost steam. The school struggled with debt and even with attempts to pay the faculty. John resigned early in the 1893 school year, saying he wanted to go back to preaching.

Was the grief of losing his wife too much for him or was it due to troubles at the college?

Or perhaps it was a difference of philosophy. Baseball mania had taken over everywhere and the Texas Baseball League formed in 1888. Fort Worth jumped on the bandwagon with their semi-pro team, the Fort Worth Panthers (later shortened to the Cats). Apparently a *Fort Worth Gazette* article ran claiming a team from Polytechnic would play the Panthers on September 23, 1893.

On September 16, there was a correction: "The Polytechnic College is strictly a Christian institution and has no organized baseball sporting club, and will have none under its present administration."

John was soon looking for a pulpit to preach from.

Rev. Lloyd took over as president of Polytechnic. At the time, he was on staff at Mulkey Methodist Church and they continued to pay his salary even though he worked at the college full time. He, in turn, paid the faculty out of his own money during the worst times. Many colleges had to move or fold when the economy faltered so badly. This was the first but not the last time when the commitment of church leaders would keep things going at Polytechnic.

Rev. John W. Adkisson
Official
Presidential
Portrait

Courtesy, Texas Wesleyan University Special Collections.

The Ghost

Annie Adkisson gave the school the last of her dwindling energy. Yet, her given name is hard to find in the college annals. She is referred to only as the president's wife or Mrs. Adkisson.

Reports of a ghost began around 1955 after long-time theatre professor Mason Johnson spotted an apparition sitting close to him during a rehearsal of *Brigadoon*. Once observed, he began seeing her with regularity. After his initial shock, he described her as "a sort of a friend,"[2] and "it has on some sort of homespun dress, by this it's a loose-like fabric that falls to the floors. I've seen it standing also, and would say it's Victorian or 1890s style."

This description comes from a theatre person who would certainly know and recognize period dress.

These occurrences were in the Ann Waggoner building—a structure sitting where the original building was built in 1891, the one that had the Adkisson's presence as part and parcel of the building. Even more interesting is an account from 1991. The original building had burned and was scheduled for demolition. The second floor had been destroyed and a fence placed around the ruin. Jim Anderson, a security guard, took some pictures and when they were developed, lo and behold a woman stood at a second floor window, waving.

Mason Johnson may have called the ghost "Georgia," but a more appropriate name may be "Annie."

Cemetery located on Texas Wesleyan campus at the corner of Bishop and Vickery. *Author's photo.*

TWO
ENTRANCE REQUIREMENTS

When a young man or woman left their homes for Polytechnic College, they still had to go through the admission process even as a returning student.

But don't worry. No one was turned away.

For a young person coming from a farm or small town, move-in day must have been quite overwhelming. During the early days, many students arrived by train. "Descending from the chugging train, the freshman clutches his trunk. The air is full of ashy fumes... The freshman walks a couple of miles before reaching the house... The small room is scantily furnished but the freshman makes do." This description comes from a student at Indiana University in 1857, but the conditions were similar for those students found at Polytechnic.

Incoming students at Polytechnic spent their initial three days in examinations. Their first college experience was to pour out all the knowledge they had in "English Grammar, Arithmetic, Algebra (through equations of the first degree), Caesar's Gallic Wars, Goodwin's Greek Grammar and Leighton's Greek Lessons."[1] Latin was in there too, for good measure.

That was just to be admitted to the freshman class. If you could not show adequate preparation, you could enroll in those classes as a preparatory student and be a "Sub-freshman." The lucky applicant who chose a Bachelor of Science did not have to take as much Greek.

Part of the admission process was the matter of the student's character. If a faculty person knew the pupil personally, they could provide a recommendation. If the student was unknown on campus, they were expected to provide a "testimonial" from their pastor (which meant they had to be church-going back home) and "one or two substantial citizens."

Returning students were tested as well to prove they were prepared enough to move up to any upper level classes. If a student wanted to take classes without pursuing a degree, they were allowed to do so as long as they were ready. Often students just wanted to take business and music classes to get them ready for other goals.

Polytechnic took pride in its Methodist roots and felt religious studies were part of being a well-educated person. At least they were up front about the mission aspect of their school. "The president and professors do all in their power to make Christians out of the students but there is no effort to proselyte them to the Methodist faith." They could afford to be magnanimous. "Methodism has never found it necessary to draw from other folds in order to swell her own numbers."

Gradually Polytechnic followed a national trend to standardize their entrance requirements and curriculum. Colleges popped up everywhere between 1870 and 1910. Thanks to money being made with new industries and businesses, endowments flourished. People had more money to spend and more time to spend it. In the universal drive to make their children's lives better than their own, parents were anxious to educate them.

All this growth did not mean colleges knew *what* to teach. The old Ivy League models focusing on literature, history, and Greek and Latin did not meet the needs of those who wanted to take over a family business or start one of their own. To keep up with these changes, Polytechnic jumped on board. They wanted to be part of the dynamic energy of their growing city of Fort Worth and the business-centric region of North Texas.

Purists to the college ideal were not happy. Their definition of a well-educated person did not include bookkeeping, for crying out loud. So those fancy colleges got together and created the Association of American Universities. This group would lead to national standards which not only provided a model for colleges; preparatory schools would now have an idea of how to prepare their students for college.

Within a few years of opening, Polytechnic revised their entrance requirements to include more subjects. Those exams on the first days of the term now included geography, history (U. S. and world), government, Latin, biology, and geometry along with literature, mathematics, and Greek.

Once classes began in earnest, what were they like?

Much different than today. According to the Indiana University student who described his experiences as "the freshman," he told it this way: "In the classroom, he sits erect, shoulder-to-shoulder on a bench…As lecture begins, the professor calls upon the [student]. With a deep breath, he stands and recites from memory a lesson he had studied the night before. After an hour of algebra, students bee-line to their next class and the routine of lecture and recitation proceeds for English literature and then again for physical geography."

Male and female students attended the same classes and sat on opposite sides of the classroom. This was no finishing school. The women got the same drill as the men.

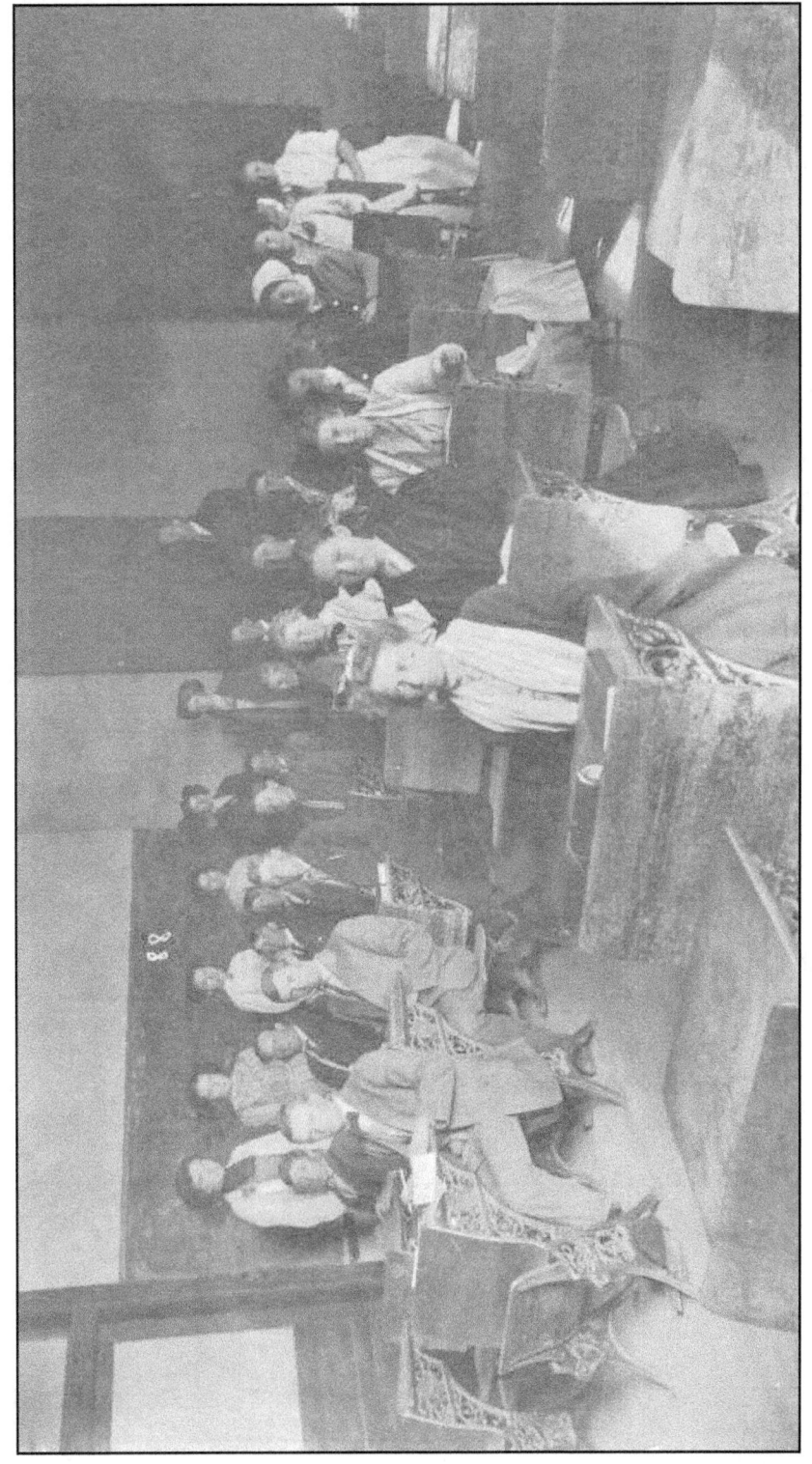

Classes were conducted with boys on one side and girls on the other.
Courtesy, Salado Public Library

In an early *Polytechnic Catalogue*, a young woman wrote a description of life on campus. The frequent reference about "recitation" during free time shows the model of students reciting from textbooks was still an established practice, even in Texas!

In spite of, or perhaps because of the rigors of college life, everyone had a spirit of optimism about their future. A newspaper item showed up in the Stephenville paper about a car loaded with students and a banner on the side of it that said "Bound for Polytechnic: A start in the right direction."

Back to our Indiana University student: he, along with everyone else, looked forward to Commencement Day, especially the speeches made by students—"every one of whom their friends expected would be President or Senator (and) of course never anything less than a representative in Congress."

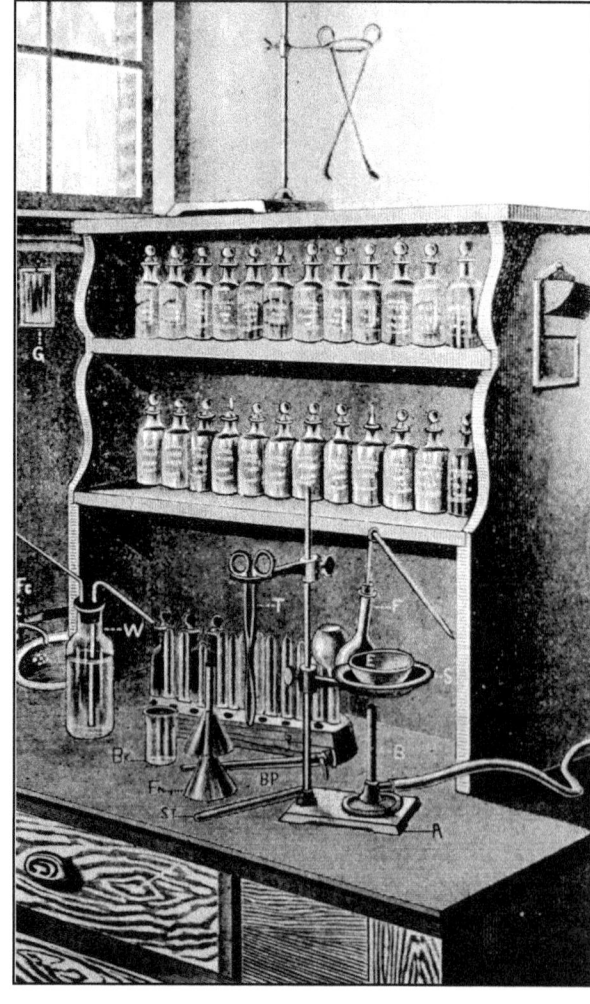

Drawing of chemistry lab at Polytechnic.

Illustration from *Polytechnic Catalogue* 1891

Courtesy, Texas Wesleyan University Special Collections.

THREE

HOW MUCH DID IT COST?

From the beginning, Bishop Key and the other organizers of Polytechnic College wanted to keep the cost of an education affordable. If someone wanted an education, money should not keep them from it. Administrators did not limit this principle to students with a degree plan. If someone wanted to take private music or foreign language lessons, individual classes that would help them in their job or business, the affordable prices applied to these students as well.

A full-time college student incurred the most cost. They paid tuition and cost of boarding in advance for the whole semester. As the decade progressed, some of these fees could be paid by the month but tuition was always paid up front. In 1891, the total bill came to about $100 per term: board $75, tuition $20, and laundry $8. In 1901, tuition and board were the same but there was a series of more fees so a student was more likely to spend between $125 and $140.

Students could keep their costs down by going home over the weekend, reducing the board to $65 and with no fee for laundry. If a student's family home was close to the campus, they could live there and simply pay tuition. Street cars began as mule-drawn coaches and upgraded quickly to electric street cars with reduced rates for everyday commuters.

From the beginning, there were also full-time preparatory students who paid the same for the boarding hall and laundry, but tuition was $15 per term.

Of course there were the extras. Private lessons for voice or instruments were $25 per term, but there was a $5 fee to use an instrument for practice. Private elocution classes were $17.50. Drawing was $15, but painting was $25. French and German lessons were $4 per month, but Spanish was $10 for a half term. For students who wanted to sing in the choir, they could do so for a moderate (undisclosed) fee.

Then came the business classes. It appears they were more likely to be taken one or two at a time. A student could take stenography—the Pencil System—at $5 per month. No indication if the school provided the pencils, but it is unlikely. If students needed the class for a whole term, that would cost a whopping $40.

Because Polytechnic was a Methodist school, they made provisions for its pastors. For those who had been licensed to preach, the tuition was waived with just a $4 matriculation fee upon entering as long as they continued to preach after college. If these youngsters did not plan to preach upon graduation, they were expected to pay tuition. If a student thought they were going to preach and then did not, they were expected to pay back that waived tuition.

Of all the special deals, the best perk was for the pastors' kids. They attended tuition-free, no matter what they did upon graduation. The Sensabaughs took advantage of this plan and Leon went first into business before finding his way back to church work.

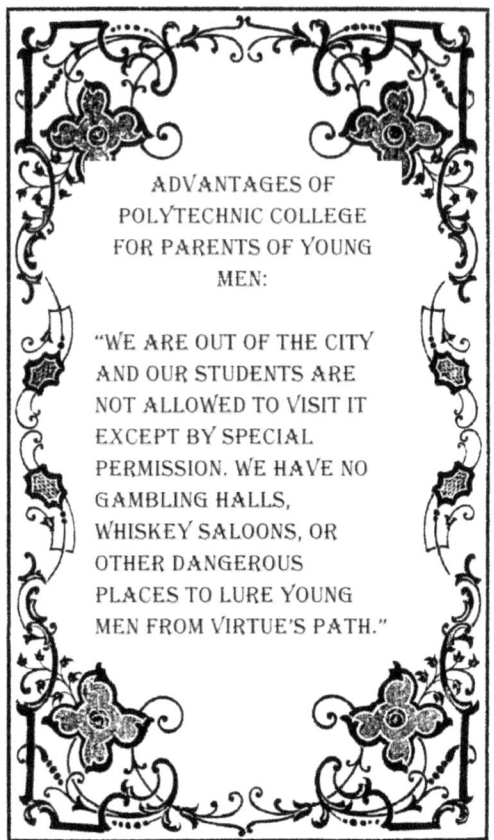

ADVANTAGES OF POLYTECHNIC COLLEGE FOR PARENTS OF YOUNG MEN:

"WE ARE OUT OF THE CITY AND OUR STUDENTS ARE NOT ALLOWED TO VISIT IT EXCEPT BY SPECIAL PERMISSION. WE HAVE NO GAMBLING HALLS, WHISKEY SALOONS, OR OTHER DANGEROUS PLACES TO LURE YOUNG MEN FROM VIRTUE'S PATH."

Surprisingly, there was a special discount for boarding facilities if families or communities sent five or more students to Polytechnic. No wonder the roll is full of students with the same last name. If female students did not live with family while at school, they lived on campus. Male students could live in approved boarding facilities off campus, but they needed to check to see if the boarding house where they put a deposit was on the approved list. To live on campus, pupils had to provide testimonials about their habits and character.

All students were required to bring their own personal care items, one pillow, a pair of pillowcases, two blankets, one quilt, a napkin, napkin rings, and an individual knife, fork, and spoon.

A special note: if feather beds were preferred, students were required to furnish them.

Courtesy, Texas Wesleyan University Special Collections.

FOUR
PROFILE: C. L. BROWNING

The first graduate from Polytechnic College was Caleb Leonidas Browning, called C. L. Browning most places, and may have been called Lee by those close to him.

C. L. would keep close ties with Polytechnic, both teaching Philosophy and Religion and remaining active in the alumni association. He played third base on the faculty baseball team in a fundraiser pitting students against faculty.

C. L. married a few months after he graduated. He and Eula May presided over many church congregations and a passel of kids. For a time he was the president of Willie Halsell College in Vinita, Oklahoma, a school in the Indian territory providing education on the reservation. Will Rogers graduated from Willie Halsell in the mid-1890s and made a name for himself, but he had already left before the Brownings' arrival in early 1900s.

C. L. ended up in San Antonio, where eventually he retired from the ministry. His congregation renamed the church in his name: Browning (now United) Methodist Church. Not satisfied with retired life, C. L. sold insurance until he died at age 93.

C. L. Browning
Courtesy, Texas Wesleyan University Special Collections

His son, C. L. Jr., was a successful businessman in San Antonio. He married Elisabeth Ewing and, with her help, began a construction company in the 1930s, building mainly houses. In the 40s, they had enough money to buy a large tract of land in Blanco County. Now known as the CL Browning ranch, the environmental research facility is run by C. L. and Elisabeth's daughter, Betsy.

A mule-drawn streetcar, like this one in Houston in the late 1870s, provided transportation to Polytechnic. The hill leading to the college was so steep, passengers often had to push the streetcar to make it up the incline.

Photograph: Public Domain

FIVE
FACULTY

Keeping the students in line must have been a taxing job for the faculty. There were so many rules! Yet, Leon Sensabaugh said the student body had high regard for the faculty, and he expressed affection and respect for them. "They did their job well and many a boy and girl shared the ideals and vision which they set."[1]

The trustees are credited with finding and hiring the best faculty of the day. Adkisson was well-connected with other colleges as well as the Methodist Conference. While qualified faculty seemed to go from campus to campus, he actually found good faculty close by.

The first graduate, C. L. Browning, worked on his Master's while teaching math and science the first year at Polytechnic. He always remained committed to helping the school in any way he could.

While J. W. Adkisson hired his kids to teach everywhere he went, they were all outstanding in their own way, especially Noble Adkisson. His curriculum vitae included Central College, University of Louisville, and Vanderbilt. He would later attend Southern Methodist University and earn a Master's degree in 1927. His thesis, about teaching a physics program, was described as a unique piece of work. He made a name for himself instructing chemistry at the College of Industrial Arts in Denton, which would later become Texas Women's College.

Professor W. F. Mister and his wife Kate were well-known educators in the area. They opened a private school in Plano and ran it for twenty years. They moved to the Polytechnic area and opened a private school there before Professor Mister was recruited to teach at the college. Mrs. Mister followed shortly after and managed the primary school. They spent another twenty years at Polytechnic and were lauded "for their thoroughness in teaching and in their uniform consistency in spiritual walks of every day life."[2]

Professor James F. Sigler was a Cornell graduate with a Master's in English Language and Literature. In the college yearbook, he is described as a teacher of rare culture and marked ability. His loyalty to Polytechnic was also praised. Since he died in his early fifties, this description seems especially poignant as he gave his best years to the struggling organization.

Professor C. B. Farrington (no connection to Fort Worth's stadium, Farrington Field) earned a degree from Vanderbilt before coming to Polytechnic to teach science. He married Gladys Busby, who was on the roll as a student at Poly.

A case of teacher/student romance?

It seemed to be accepted because President Lloyd performed their marriage ceremony. They left after three years, and Professor Farrington then taught at Sam Houston State College for thirty-five years until he retired. He has a building named in his honor on that campus, and Leon Sensabaugh named Professor Farrington one of his favorite teachers at Polytechnic.

There were multiple students who returned to teach at their Alma Mater. Josie Crutchfield taught music in 1892-93. Fred Newsom was principal of the sub-freshmen for 1896-97. Emma Ray taught art from 1897-99, then again from 1902-06. E. P. Hall, before he became "Doc" Hall, taught Anatomy and Physiology in 1901-02. Philo Ingraham, before he became a customs agent, went through the Business program and taught from 1901-03.

Faculty 1898

Standing left to right: Mrs. W.F. Mister, Shannon, C.B. Farrington, R.B. McSwain, B.S. Brown, Mrs J.F. Sigler
Seated left to right: W.F. Mister, unknown, President W.F. Lloyd, Mrs. W.F. Lloyd, J.F. Sigler

Courtesy, Texas Wesleyan University Special Collections (Maud Hunter Collection).

SIX

PROFILE: T. L. RIPPEY

The second Polytechnic graduate was T. L. Rippey, who went by Lee, and his life took quite a surprising turn.

Since C. L. Browning graduated with a Master's, Lee Rippey actually holds the first Bachelor's Degree awarded by Polytechnic. Lee was part of a large family whose patriarch was W. M. P. Rippey, a pastor of some renown as a preacher and temperance "pioneer of the crusade against saloons." The senior Rippey campaigned for prohibition in Alabama, not backing down even when threatened by some "ruffians." Lee was eleven or twelve when this happened.

The Rippey family was quite invested in Polytechnic. Lee's father gave the commencement speech the year Lee graduated in 1893, and his sister Lula was the art professor there.

Lee followed in his father's footsteps and served in many churches in Texas and Oklahoma, even taking leadership positions in the Oklahoma Conference. He married a woman named Mamie Kircher. Her father came from Germany and her mother from the Alsace region of France. The Texas town of Castroville has a large Alsace community, but a connection to Mamie is unknown.

In 1910, Lee requested an assignment in the West for his health. Usually code for tuberculosis, the outcome could have been quite grim for his family that now included three children. Records show that he received treatment at the Battle Creek Sanitarium.

The Battle Creek Sanitarium was run by the Kellogg brother of cereal fame in Battle Creek, Michigan. Called "San" for short, the facility offered a wide array of medical treatments "to heal the whole person by caring for the mind, body and spirit…abstinence from alcohol and tobacco, as well as moderation in diet, work and the use of pharmaceutical drugs. The patients were taught to care for themselves whenever possible using 'natural' means, including water, sunshine, exercise, rest and proper diet."[1] The San had an impressive track record in curing difficult cases, even surgical ones. Lee would have been in the new building, which had been rebuilt after a fire and dedicated in 1903. It was a six-story brick with a Beaux Art design. How could a lowly Methodist minister afford a treatment like this? It appears his fortunes had changed.

On November 4, 1913, the *Ada Weekly News* ran this headline:

"REV. T. L. RIPPEY MAKES FORTUNE."

What a lead!

"REV. T. L. RIPPEY, FORMERLY PASTOR OF ST. PAUL'S CHURCH, HAS MADE $100,000 IN MINING TRANSACTIONS IN MONTANA."

That relocation for his health put him in line to make some money. "By the right sort of investments, he came in possession of valuable stock that made him a snug fortune."

In 1916, those investments parlayed into mineral rights and half ownership of a patent for a rock drill. At Polytechnic he was known for elocution and music, not science, so his contribution to this invention is unclear. However, he is in the annals of history with the patent.

By the time his partner filed for this patent, Lee had relocated to Dallas and lived out his days there. Records show that Mamie's mother and sister lived with them in Dallas in 1920. Lee died in 1961 at the age of 89.

Apparently the cure worked.

Battle Creek Sanitarium
Courtesy, The Willard Library Collection (Public Domain)

T. L. "Lee" Rippey and his wife, Mamie
Courtesy, Texas Wesleyan Special Collections (Maud Hunter Collection).

Men's Dormitory, 1902.
When the dormitory was replaced, this structure was moved
a few streets from the campus and became an orphanage.
Courtesy, Texas Wesleyan University Special Collections (Maud Hunter Collection).

SEVEN

PROFILE: EDWIN SPURLOCK

Being a working parent and going to school is not unique to the twenty-first century. E. L. Spurlock, or Edwin, did all of that at Polytechnic. A trained minister, he was hired to supervise the boys' dormitory. He and his family, wife Mary and sons Claton and Lawrence (also called Lonnie), could have lived in the dorm because that was common for college personnel. The boys attended the preparatory school while Edwin worked on his degree.

The young men residents of the dorm nicknamed him "Boss." Edwin reported that even after he left the school, if former students saw him in public, they still called him "Boss." Edwin said his memories of Polytechnic were dominated by being in a perpetual state of exhaustion. Once he got everyone settled by curfew, he then did his own school work.

Leon Sensabaugh wrote that he would sneak out of the dorm after curfew if he wanted to do something in town. Was the long-suffering Boss too tired to notice any shenanigans or simply too tired to chase them down?

Edwin remained in higher education, spending much of his career in Sherman at Kidd-Key College. He was business manager for fourteen years and its president for five. His son Claton died in 1900 at age fifteen, and then his wife died in 1907. Things looked up when he met and married May Carver, herself a widow.

Kidd-Key school had an interesting history with names familiar to Polytechnic. Methodist Episcopal Bishop Joseph Key is the "Key" in Kidd-Key, but became involved in the school in a roundabout way. When the bishop found himself a widower, he became smitten with Lucy Ann Kidd. Lucy was born in Kentucky before the Civil War and was raised in a genteel fashion emphasizing an education in the classics and fine arts. She married Dr. Henry Kidd of Mississippi, but the war and her husband's lingering illness and death left her with three small children and debt. She became a principal and teacher at Whitworth College. This work led her to be a front-runner for the presidency at the North Texas Female College in Sherman.

Not that it was a plum job. The college was in debt and had been closed for two years. In order to revitalize the school, she traveled throughout Texas and the Indian Territory (now Oklahoma) recruiting students, money, and backing. Thanks to her efforts, she opened the school in September with 100 students and enrollment continued to grow.

Lucy got them in good enough financial shape they could buy land and buildings from a close-by defunct college. She married the good bishop Key in 1892 and hyphenated her name before it was the thing to do.

Lucy was on a roll now. She expanded the music department so the school was deemed North Texas Female College and the Kidd-Key Conservatory of Music. She recruited music faculty from Europe and all over the United States. One of her recruits, Carl Venth, was a violinist who would expand his career to Polytechnic and Texas Women's College. Lucy firmly believed that her students should become ladies and insisted on ladylike behavior. Her strict regulations led to a decline in enrollment as World War I loomed.

Then another blow was dealt when the Methodist church put most of their big money into Southern Methodist University in 1915 and pulled back from all the little colleges under its watch, including Polytechnic and Kidd-Key. She died in 1916 before the college buckled to society pressures and the Great Depression.

The "boss" Edwin remained at Kidd-Key until 1928 when he resigned due to illness. He would die four years later at a home in Dallas close to SMU.

Lucy Kidd-Key,
President of
Kidd-Key College,
Sherman, Tx.

Courtesy, Texas Wesleyan University Special Collections (Maud Hunter Collection).

EIGHT
RULES FOR GIRLS

Looking at the rules of Polytechnic students, especially the rules for women, with a twenty-first century perspective makes the environment seem overly restrictive, even repressive. The school's organizers were church leaders in a time of social change and they took their job seriously: molding the next generation of leaders. These young men graduates would lead churches, businesses, and communities; women were leaders in their homes and, by extension, society. With a strong educational and religious foundation, the future would indeed be in capable hands.

Some of the Polytechnic students were quite young, too. The word "college" usually just meant "private school," often including a preparatory school and admitting students as young as fourteen or fifteen if they could pass the entrance exam and had letters of recommendation. In Fort Worth of the 1890s, there was no public school system. A school like Polytechnic was a welcome alternative to paying a tutor or doing without education at all.

There was a lack of national academic standards, which is another reason the Southern Methodist Episcopals were compelled to get in the education business. They made it up as they went. Everyone did. After 1900, the Association of American Universities tried to create some guidelines. There was a hot debate about whether programs such as business and agriculture were scholarly enough to include in a college. Polytechnic came down on the side that the fast-growing community of Fort Worth, with it robust business sector, would need educated workers. Because of this, they included business courses in the class offerings. The older Methodist university, Southwestern in Georgetown, scoffed at what we call "vocational" courses and kept their ideals lofty.

Polytechnic's name says it all. It means "many arts," including the practical ones.

Educating women was becoming part of the social change of the nineteenth century as well. More and more families gravitated to a "separate spheres" doctrine. A woman's world "was the world of privacy, family and morality while man's sphere was the public world—economic striving, political maneuvering, and social competition."[1] Women became more adept at making a difference in their communities by influencing through their home, their families, and their churches. Some female-centric reform efforts led to improvements in penitentiaries, asylums, and schools as well as the creation of temperance societies.

Within this framework, it should be no surprise that female enrollment at Polytechnic was as high as men. In the first decade they counted more female graduates than male. Some of those degrees were from a program known as Mistress of English Literature, which was a shortened program but prepared them to teach or write for the expanding journalism field.

A dormitory was provided for men early in Polytechnic's life, but they were allowed to live off campus, relying on street cars to bring them to class. The young women were expected to live on campus. During Polytechnic's inaugural year, the young women lived with the president under the watchful eye of Mrs. Adkisson until the boarding hall was finished. This must have resulted in a lot of cooking for Annie.

Young men were expected to wear dark suits. Women paid for their uniforms by buying the fabric and taking it to the same seamstress in town.

A student wrote a description of life in the female dorm for the 1895 *Bulletin*. They were awakened at 6 a.m. by a "melodious (?) gong." The question mark is telling. By the time another gong sounded an hour later, they'd better be dressed and have their rooms tidied. At that time, they lined up to wait for the dorm matron to give them the signal to come downstairs. In the breakfast room, they stood behind their chairs until a Bible passage had been read and prayers said. No mention of how fast they ate or how much they talked.

The women had an hour to get ready for school. The student author gives some suggestions: "...curl their bangs, braid their hair, wash their hands, change their dress, polish their shoes, put on a clean apron, look over their lessons." Then each segment of the morning had its assigned classes until lunch.

After lunch was "gesture class" for a whole hour, designed around practice exercises and movements to give ladies the "grace of one of the ancient Greeks." They had a sort of free period where they could practice recitations or musical instruments or perhaps paint or draw. Chapel at 3:30, after which was a break until dinner (similar routine as breakfast). There was an hour after dinner. Again with the suggestions: "one might walk, gather flowers or commune with nature."

Evening schedules for the women were also carefully planned. Friday evenings were the exception and the highlight. Prayer meetings included the men, but they were not allowed to speak to each other. Two or three times a year, males and females were allowed to talk to each other, but only under the "watchful eyes of the faculty."

Because school discipline bred self-discipline, these rules were strictly enforced. Still, that cheekiness in the student's article makes it seem that students found a way to have some fun, too.

In an interview, Ladye Dennis Hall, class of 95 (1895, that is) was asked what the students did for entertainment when she was a pupil. She talked about the occasional Open House where the boys and girls could see each other.

"But they were strict in those days," she added, "and tried to keep us apart."

Then, with that merry twinkle in her eyes she said, "It didn't work."

Ladye met her husband E. P. there. Eva Hall (95) met her husband J. P. Leach. Marvin Coppedge (95) met his wife Ada. Matthew Blanton married Beall Sawyer (96).

Those are just a few of the matches made at Polytechnic.

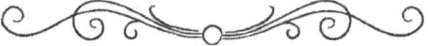

Women's Dorm Room
Courtesy, Texas Wesleyan University Special Collections.

Beall Sawyer (looking down) and classmates.
Courtesy, Private Collection of the Ellis and Blanton Families.

NINE

PROFILE: ROLAND BROOKS AND WESSIE ADKISSON

Just because male and female student were not allowed to mingle, sparks still flew.

Even among the faculty!

Wessie Adkisson, President J. W. and Annie's daughter, was one of the original professors at Polytechnic, teaching elocution. She is listed as an elocution instructor at Central College in 1890, the school her father led before coming to Polytechnic. In 1893, *Werner Magazine* published a glowing critique of her production *The Angels of Buena Vista*:

> "The Polytechnic is taking a leading position in regard to elocution, largely through the efforts of Miss Adkisson."

Then along came Roland Brooks. Trained at Emory University, he graduated and was quickly hired by Polytechnic to teach Latin and Greek. He had a strong background in mathematics. Maybe Wessie liked the way his numbers added up; maybe Roland liked how she said her words.

They married in December 1895. Their son, Candler, was born the following September while they were still in Fort Worth. At the end of the school term, they moved to Alabama and then Georgia, Roland's home.

Sadly, Wessie died in 1905 when she was only twenty-seven and Candler was nine. Roland married again three years later to Jane Lewis. They had a son together and named him Charles. Roland was the superintendent of schools for twenty years before he died in 1937.

Candler went on to graduate from the Georgia Institute of Technology, but eventually put his own math skills to work as an officer in a bank in Naples, Florida.

Arch Hall
Courtesy, Texas Wesleyan University Special Collections.

TEN

PROFILE: THE HALL FAMILY

What happened after Arch Hall and his brother W. D. gave the land for the Methodist college?

All their kids went to school there, of course.

As a Confederate soldier, W. D. Hall had been captured, held in a Union prison camp, and spent time there studying Latin. Once he and his brother settled on their homestead, they set up a school for their kids and anyone close enough to use it. Along with their relatives, the Tandys, their part of the area began to look like a town complete with a school, stores, even a blacksmith. The Halls continued their commitment to education, not only by supporting the college but also by staying active in public schools. Their dedication to education was backed up with action.

Little wonder that on the first Polytechnic roll, both of W. D.'s sons were included. Edward—also known as E. S., and Charles—also known as Charlie, registered with the first class. E. S. would later appear as a trustee for the Polytechnic Schools.

Arch's kids rounded out the Hall part of the alphabetical listing. After all, their homestead had a college in the backyard! John Rogers, or Harris as some of the family called him, was at Polytechnic fresh from Missouri Military Academy. He graduated with a music degree in 1895, performing a duet with his sister Eva during their commencement program.

Eva met her future husband Hubert at Polytechnic. She graduated in 1895, and with a dual degree in Literature and Music, she was quite the star of the commencement program. Not only did she perform a duet with John, she even sang a solo and read her essay "Ministry of Music," possibly representing the Susan Key Literary Society since she had been an officer their inception year. When Hubert graduated in 1896, they were the first couple to marry in the Polytechnic Methodist chapel.

At the same commencement program, Hubert won a medal for his oration on "Definite Labor: The Key to Success," possibly as a representative of the Philosophians. From Polytechnic, he went on to Fort Worth Medical College. He owned a private practice in his hometown Aledo before opening the first hospital in Weatherford.

Ladye Dennis, whose family settled in Farmer's Branch, Texas, came to Polytechnic during those same years and graduated in that same class. She was particularly keen to study with a professor at Polytechnic. She found a man who caught her eye: one of the Halls. Ewin.

In an interview when she was in her eighties, Ladye said it was customary to wait until after school to get married so she and Ewin waited, which is ironic since Eva didn't. While Ewin went to Fort Worth Medical College with his Polytechnic alumnus and now brother-in-law Hubert, Ladye returned to Farmer's Branch and taught school until he finished. They married in 1900 and Ewin had a robust medical practice in Polytechnic and Fort Worth. After that, he was known simply as "Doc." He was the third person in Polytechnic to have a telephone, only preceded by the pastor of Polytechnic Methodist and the college.

Doc, like all his family, believed in giving back to the community. The Hall family left their mark whether in Polytechnic or Fort Worth, Aledo or Weatherford. As an active Mason, Doc treated the orphans at the Masonic Home free of charge. He became even more involved as the school's football team began a crazy winning streak, thanks to a coach named Rusty Russell.

Called the "Mighty Mites," teams from the Masonic Home were fearless, maybe even reckless. Doc never missed a game and was often at practice. When no one else believed in them, Rusty and Doc were partners in molding the players into a team even though the boys were smaller than any of their competitors and fewer in numbers than the city teams. They went to games in an old blue pick-up that could barely get them down the road. They made do with their limited resources.

Doc had his hands full keeping them healthy and ready to play, but he and the rest of the country got caught up in the dream. In the 30s and 40s, when the country went through some of its darkest times, the little orphans were the perpetual underdogs who kept playing, kept fighting against all those bigger players and outmaneuvered them with better, innovative plays. It was their heart that caught the nation's attention and Doc was always there, on the sideline for every game. Just in case someone got hurt.

And someone always got hurt.

W. D. Hall
Courtesy, Texas Wesleyan University Special Collections.

Doc Hall (seated next to A.H. Odom) in later years at a Masonic Hall football game in 1941. *Courtesy, Fort Worth Star-Telegram Collection, Special Collections, The University of Texas at Arlington Libraries.*

Eva Hall Leach, the father Arch Hall, E.P. Hall (Doc) and Harris Hall; circa 1925.
Courtesy of Gene Leon Leonard.

ELEVEN

PROFILE: THE TANDY FAMILY

On the rolls for 1891 and 1892, the names Annie and Fanny Tandy appear. No, they were not twins, but cousins.

Roger and Mary Tandy were Kentucky pioneers who settled along the banks of the Sycamore Creek. Roger created Tandy Lake from waters of the creek. Even as early as the 1880s it was a popular recreation area. As their son George matured, he took over managing the land and ranch. George was the one who donated the land to Polytechnic College with the Hall brothers, who were related by marriage. The combined efforts of these two families supported financial development of all kinds, including the establishment of a cotton mill on the east side.

Even in its early years, Fort Worth was shaped by the Tandys' influence. In this case, east Fort Worth. The family could have been a draw to another Tandy's influence. Charles Tandy would make a huge mark on the city thanks to a leather goods and an electronics company.

Many of George's children would show up on the Polytechnic roll.

But this was 1891. George's oldest daughter Annie was at the new Polytechnic taking piano lessons and elocution classes. Active in the local Methodist church with the Latimer family, Annie caught the eye of Henry. Quick as a wink, she was married and no longer at Polytechnic.

Alongside Annie was Fanny. Fanny's father, Archibald Tandy, had not settled in Fort Worth, but went further west to Haskell, almost to the Texas Panhandle. He established a big ranch and sent his oldest to the new college his relatives helped start. In all likelihood, Fanny lived with her relations while she was in school.

Back home in Haskell, Samuel Scott was quietly building his own big ranch. Descended from veterans of the Texas Revolution, his Virginian ancestors served in the U. S. War for Independence. Sam was raised in Georgetown, his father being one of the founders of the other Southern Methodist college in Texas, Southwestern. He studied hard and received his A.B. (the equivalent of a Bachelor's) from the hometown college before he was eighteen.

Lured by the siren call of the ranching business, Sam moved to Haskell. Not content with managing from afar, Sam immersed himself in the business. He worked his cattle as a cowboy, living in lime camp dugouts.

He rode the line, stood night guard in severe storms and blazing heat and round-ups. He rode the range so much he wore out horses and had to frequently get fresh ones.

Four years of that was enough. He went back to Georgetown and got a law degree. Once he passed the bar, he returned to Haskell to continue building his empire, buying more land, accumulating stock in the Haskell National Bank and an interest in the phone company.

Fanny was going to college during some of this time. She was a nice Methodist girl going to the new Methodist college. She knew a good thing when she saw it.

How could she resist a man rugged enough to punch cows and smart enough to pass the bar? And Sam was a strong Methodist as well. He was elected a lay delegate to the general conference.

They made a good life in Haskell, later moving to San Antonio, getting involved in Southwestern College's politics about the time there was tension between Southwestern and Polytechnic. It is doubtful any of their children went to Polytechnic.

Lewis Tandy, Annie's brother, would join the ranks at Polytechnic in 1901. Although he was active in sports and the literary society, he was a quiet presence in the college's first decade so his story will be saved for later.

George Tandy
Courtesy, Texas Wesleyan University Special Collections.

Painting of Tandy Lake
Courtesy of the Tandy family.

This painting by Berniece Leach hung in the Polytechnic church for many years. Notice the college building in the background.
Courtesy, Texas Wesleyan University Special Collections.

TWELVE

RELIGIOUS FERVOR

Religious life was an inescapable part of Polytechnic life, but the students' lives away from campus reflected this dedication to the church. Although most were Methodist, students attended other churches as well. The admissions process with its requirement of character testimonials almost guaranteed students had a home church. To devote their Friday nights to prayer meeting was not a sacrifice, but a given.

Even if Saturday was relatively unscheduled for each to pursue their own interests, come 7:30 Saturday evening they were meant to get back on track. That time slot was dedicated to preparing for the next day's Sunday School lesson. Since the religious atmosphere was similar to home, it may have quelled feelings of homesickness.

October was time for the yearly college revival. In addition to the Polytechnic Methodist minister, other well-known speakers appeared. There was perhaps music to prepare. Classes would be canceled and assignments postponed. There was excitement in the air. In the student publication, *The Polytechnician*, the sermons were reported to be powerful, thought-provoking, and emotional experiences.

Leon Sensabaugh remembered everyone on campus enjoying the revivals. "Indeed, we requested that there be at least two revivals each year, one in the fall and one in the spring."

We Must Educate ✦ ✦ ✦

But we must bear in mind that there are many ways of obtaining an education outside of the school-room. Among these,

TRAVEL

HOLDS A CONSPICUOUS PLACE.

By its excellent service, has greatly reduced the tediousness of travel making it a

POSITIVE LUXURY.

PERFECT WAGNER BUFFET SLEEPING-CAR SERVICE

BETWEEN

CHICAGO,

ST. LOUIS,

KANSAS CITY,

HANNIBAL, SEDALIA AND TEXAS POINTS.

FREE RECLINING CHAIR CARS ON ALL TRAINS

For Routes, Rates, Maps, Time Tables, or other information call on or address:

H. P. HUGHES,
General Passenger and Ticket Agent, Denison, Texas.

C. H. BOARDMAN,   **JAS. BARKER,**
T. P. A., Fort Worth, Texas.   G. P. & T. A., M. K. & T. R'y System, St. Louis, Mo.

THIRTEEN

SCHOLARSHIPS

For the fledgling university to succeed, there had to be students. Polytechnic administration was creative in ways of selling their college.

Advertisements took full advantage of the college's location: away from town where evil lurked in the form of demon liquor and gambling halls.

Fort Worth still had that dual nature. The town was so sleepy, a panther could stroll down most streets but not the streets of Hell's Half Acre. The Southern Methodist Episcopals knew how to play on a parent's fear.

Notices also offered parents and students the chance to talk to the president one-on-one. They could set up an appointment with the president himself. Rev. Adkisson, Rev. Lloyd, and others offered to come to a prospective student's home and pitch the school to the family. Edwin Spurlock reported he spent one summer traveling to surrounding towns to visit parents.

In 1895, area newspapers offered scholarships. In quite the brilliant marketing ploy, those young people who sold the most subscriptions received votes and whoever had the most votes would win a year's scholarship. The *Fort Worth Gazette* only offered the deal to young men, perhaps because they had a similar contest for an all-girls music school. In Stephenville, the contest generated quite a competition between both men and women.

Under the headline "Who will go to college free?" the paper reported each week's total votes. After the first week, Miss Dollie Marshal of Stephenville quickly became the front runner. The newspaper also ran a letter of recommendation.

> "Miss Dollie Marshal, a worthy young lady who lives about five miles east of Stephenville. She is a very intelligent girl, and would appreciate a year at college."

Articles kept interest stirred up by cautioning prospective students not to wait. "Quite a number have expressed their intention" to enter only after they see how many votes they have to beat.

A month later, Dollie had a healthy lead with seventy-eight votes. Her closest competitor was Amanda Skipper with forty-six votes. One young man withdrew from the contest, asking for his votes to go to Lurlene Smith who at this point only had twelve.

What a difference two weeks made. Dollie disappeared from the group. Lurlene's votes surged ahead to one hundred thirty-five, making her look like the sure winner with only a week to go.

Then, an unexpected turn of events!

> "Late in the afternoon and only a short while before 6 o'clock, a sealed envelope was handed in marked 'votes for Chas. Holland of Lingleville'."

The dark horse came up with no warning. He was the winner with one hundred seventy votes. No doubt Lurlene and Dollie were sorely disappointed.

Charles was listed as the assistant librarian at Polytechnic in 1896, then fades from history.

FOURTEEN

PROFILE: LIZZIE ADKISSON

Another of Annie and J. W.'s daughters, Lizzie, was one of the two first female Polytechnic graduates in 1894.

The college offered a degree called Mistress of English Literature, which did not require as many credits as a Bachelor's and focused mainly on the arts. Several of Polytechnic's early graduates were women who took advantage of this program.

Lizzie married a Waxahachie man in 1897. William Bird Forrest, who went by Bird, was a house builder. Family records show that they lived in a little house which they moved and lived in while Bird built their big, beautiful one. That house still stands and is on the National Register of Historic Places.

Lizzie always loved flowers and somehow she came up with the idea to open a little flower shop. Things really took off when Bird turned from house building to horticulture. Their shop grew and included greenhouses. *Bird Forrest's Florist* covered a city block.

A picture of the couple reveals that Bird accomplished all that with a peg leg!

Bird was on a sales call in 1931 when he had a massive heart attack. Somehow he managed to make it to the Midlothian hospital where he died.

Lizzie and Bird had six children. One of their grandsons became a well-known Hollywood character actor: Frederick (Frederic) Fenimore Forrest, known for such movies as *Apocalypse Now* and *Lonesome Dove*, in which he played the unforgettable, villainous character Blue Duck.

William Bird Forrest Home

By Renelibrary, Own Work. Wikimedia. CC BY-SA 3.0

World War I Mess Line
Camp Bowie Training Camp: Fort Worth, Texas   June 1918
Courtesy, National Archives.

FIFTEEN
PROFILE: INNIE KIDD

Innie Kidd was the other first female graduate from Polytechnic along with Lizzie Adkisson. Innie was from Waxahachie, where Lizzie went to live after she graduated. Her given name was Lorinda Ulrica Kidd, but many times she was mistakenly called Annie. When Innie married Jordan Yarborough Cumming III, she must have thought she lived a charmed life. Instead, tragedy struck far too often.

Jordan was the son of Judge C. C. Cummings. A Confederate veteran originally from Mississippi, C.C had lost a hand in the battle of Gettysburg. He practiced law in Mississippi and for some reason was attracted to the growing city of Fort Worth in 1873.

That was a big year for C.C. He married and had his firstborn within that calendar year. Three years later, he ran for county judge. As a newcomer, he faced an uphill battle but convinced the voters he was the best candidate. Under his administration, he helped establish the public school system, roads and bridges were improved, and he oversaw the building of a courthouse and jail after the existing one burned; all of this was accomplished during only two terms. He continued to practice law and follow his other passion: writing. Especially historical writing. He even helped form the Bohemian Club, a writing and book group.

Jordan seemed just as promising. When Innie married him in 1899, he was a prosecutor for Tarrant County and his name appeared in newspaper accounts of some of the area's biggest cases. Waxahachie was a prosperous little town because of the railroad, so Innie was no doubt aware of the benefits of social status. The couple lived on Cummings Street in Fort Worth, for goodness sakes!

The turning point occurred in 1918. The judge died in May. Then on September 12, Jordan and his brother Tarrant were required to register for possible military service since the U. S. had joined in the war efforts of World War I. In 1917, the Selective Service Act was passed, requiring every male from ages twenty-one to forty-five to register. Men went in three groups: group one was for men between twenty-one and thirty-one; group two for men who turned twenty-one that year; group three was for ages eighteen through forty-five. Jordan was forty-five; Tarrant was forty-two. Tarrant went joined the military at that point, but he was dead by October

24. Because he is buried in Arlington National Cemetery, it seems he was quickly killed in action.

Jordan died on December 12 from an undisclosed cause.

Fort Worth was hit hard in 1918 by the Spanish influenza and especially hard at Camp Bowie, the Army training facility about three miles west of downtown. On September 27, the headline screamed: "EIGHTY-ONE SPANISH INFLUENZA CASES AT CAMP BOWIE BASE HOSPITAL." By October 4, the camp hospital reported 1900 patients. While it is not clear if Jordan was at Camp Bowie, the entire city suffered because of this pandemic. Suddenly, the future looked drastically different for Innie.

She was left with an eighteen-year-old son and a fourteen-year-old daughter to raise alone. At some point she used that Polytechnic degree and went back to teaching.

Tragedy struck again in 1934. Innie and Jordan's daughter Ermine, who may have been Emmy or Ermmie for short, was not getting along with her husband even after their divorce. She had four children: William, eight; Mary Ermine, four; Bobby, two; and Gaye, six months old. Her twenty-four-year-old cousin, Patricia Kidd, also lived with her in Dallas. The children's father, Mike Harriss, had been granted visitation rights and could visit twice a week at "all reasonable hours."[1]

"I couldn't stand it anymore," an injured Mike Harriss told the policeman, apparently referring to the separation from his children. He begged Emmy to remarry him or give him custody of the kids. She refused on several occasions. So he showed up at her house with a gun, again demanding marriage or custody.

A servant in the kitchen heard arguing and cousin Pat must have tried to settle things down. Suddenly she cried, "Mike, don't do that!" Then there were gunshots. Emmy was shot twice and fell face-down on the couch. Pat was shot twice when she tried to escape. Mike stepped over her where she'd collapsed on the floor.

Mike called for an ambulance, telling whoever answered he had just shot two women. Then he turned the gun around and shot himself in the chest, staying alive long enough to tell the police what happened and to call his employer when he arrived at the hospital.

Three of the four children were home that day to bear witness to this crime, but the oldest one, William, was visiting his grandmother Innie in Fort Worth.

Innie would live for another twenty years to the age of eighty-one. Her death certificate listed her as a teacher.

SIXTEEN
BOARD OF TRUSTEES

Not many think about the important job of a college's board of trustees. They are the behind-the-scenes force that runs the show and makes the tough choices. What did this look like at Polytechnic? Thanks to the dedication of these men, Polytechnic survived rough waters and dark days.

Modern boards can have thirty-five to fifty members. Polytechnic had ten to fifteen. Boards do things like review academic programs, raise funds (an especially important job in 1891), approve policies, and make long-range plans. It may not be glamorous, but colleges need their trustees.

Who were the trustees for Polytechnic, and why were they so interested in its welfare? During the entire Polytechnic era, Bishop Joseph S. Key was a constant. Of course, the college was his baby, and he wanted to make sure it ran the way he wanted it to. The others were civic leaders in their own right.

Some of the business and civic leaders of the era included: Judge Alex Steadman; Texas State Representative T. T. D. Andrews; W. J. Boaz, real estate investor and owner of the Texas and Ellis Bank, which later became City National Bank; W. G. Newby, president of the American National Bank; Dr. W. H. Williams, owner/operator of Wholesale Drug Co.; and E. J. White, vice-president and general solicitor of the Missouri Pacific Railroad.

Another Fort Worth pioneer and city father was a Polytechnic trustee, George Mulkey. Mulkey was a self-made mover and shaker who took a deep interest in educational and church endeavors. He and his family were the founders of Mulkey Methodist Church, and he was a major supporter of Polytechnic. Not only did he generously provide funds to keep the school going, but his kids attended school there as well. Webb and Karl were some of the first students at the school while Homer and Young were students in the mid-1900s.

Through the years there have been a number of ministers to serve on the Board of Trustees including W. P. Wilson and W. L. Nelms, who were involved with Central College and Granbury College so they understood what colleges needed. W. H. Vaughn was the first administrator for the Methodist Home for Children. Dr. Lloyd served in multiple capacities: trustee, college president, parent of a college student. Stuart Lloyd, his son, graduated in 1900, joining other trustees' kids who attended Polytechnic.

O. F. Sensabaugh was credited with being the first Methodist minister west of the Continental Divide. Claiming one of his first sermons was in a saloon, Dr. Sensabaugh and his family moved around in Colorado and New Mexico before coming to Texas. For ten years there was at least one Sensabaugh, sometimes many Sensabaughs, on the Polytechnic rolls: Leon, George, Oscar, and Leona.

Oliver S. Kennedy moved to Fort Worth in 1877 and became active in Democratic Party politics. More notably, he platted and organized the city of Kennedale, which he named after himself. Three of the six Kennedy kids were at Polytechnic in those early days. James was active in the Philosophians, giving two speeches at the 1894 commencement exercises and receiving an award for high grades. Georgia Pearl, who went by Pearl, won a gold medal in the elocution contest that same year, in competition against five other contestants. She would graduate in 1897. The last Kennedy was Narcissa, called Narcie, and she kept a very low profile.

James B. Baker was another businessman interested in Polytechnic's well-being. Coming to Fort Worth from England, he set up Baker Brothers Nursery and kept buying land around Fort Worth to grow trees and plants for their business. Before he knew it, the family was in real estate development. Nursery catalogs dating from 1892 were mailed through Texas or delivered by James on horseback. It was a tree from Baker Brothers Nursery President Theodore Roosevelt planted in front of the downtown Fort Worth Carnegie Library when he visited in 1905.

The Baker family remained invested in Polytechnic as it changed to Texas Women's College, then later to Texas Wesleyan University. James's son, Edward, served on the Board of Trustees from 1945-1969. James's granddaughter, Louella Baker Martin, donated a house! James's house from the Riverside area was cut in two, loaded on a flatbed truck, and reassembled on the campus of Texas Wesleyan University. Louella and her husband also funded the upgrade of the auditorium in the Ann Waggoner Fine Arts Buildings to a state-of-the-art performance venue and created Lou's Place, a building that provides meeting space for banquets and receptions. Most recently, Louella has enabled the university to open its new student center.

The family legacy continues!

Dr. W. F. Lloyd and Family
*Courtesy, Texas Wesleyan University Special Collections
(Centennial Collection)*

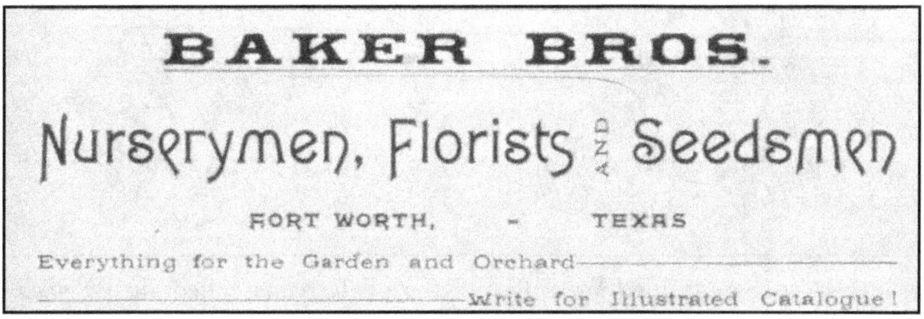

BAKER BROS.

Nurserymen, Florists and Seedsmen

FORT WORTH, - TEXAS

Everything for the Garden and Orchard——————
——————Write for Illustrated Catalogue!

The literary societies joined forces to produce a newspaper called *The Polytechnian*. E. C. Hunter's parents were dorm parents, and he died a few years after this picture was taken. *Courtesy, Texas Wesleyan University Special Collections.*

SEVENTEEN
PHILOSOPHIANS AND ADKISSONIANS: THE LITERARY SOCIETIES

As early as the first year, Polytechnic students organized literary societies. A trend on college campuses of the day, literary societies were part social outlet, part team spirit. An Indiana University student admitted his homesickness finally faded once he got involved in the literary society.

Given that the typical classroom ran on memorization and recitation, what did Polytechnic students do for fun?

More memorizing and speech making, of course. The difference was they could write their own literary works, debate topics important to them, even perform musical selections. It was how nineteenth century students could connect.

Literary societies were established on college campuses all over the country by the 1890s, so there were abundant models for the Polytechnic students to follow. The societies were all about self-improvement. In the *Manual of College Literary Societies*: "When a body of youth are brought together for the purpose of receiving a liberal education, those who are enthusiastic and ambitious immediately seek helps for their self-improvement, especially in rhetorical and literary exercises."

This was primarily done over and over again by public speaking, the constant practicing thought to be a good way to achieve "the highest possible degree of 'mental, moral and social' improvement." These were lofty goals for any college student, but particularly for the large numbers of students who were ministers or aspiring ministers at Polytechnic.

The equal emphasis on debate played a valuable role in critical thinking. Since classes were not the freewheeling discussions that characterize contemporary classes, literary societies gave students the chance to look at issues from multiple viewpoints. The society could be considered a "safe space" for trying out ideas.

Back to the *Manual*: "When the faculties of youth are in an immature state and their knowledge scanty, crude and imperfectly arranged, if they are prematurely hurried into a habit of fluent speaking, they are in danger of retaining through life a careless habit of pouring forth ill-digested thoughts in well turned phrases, and an aversion to exhaustive research."

The Adkissonians
Courtesy, Texas Wesleyan University Special Collections.

The Philosophians
Courtesy, Texas Wesleyan University Special Collections.

Even in the nineteenth century, college was criticized for not providing for all of a student's needs. "The tendency of our popular institutions is to encourage readiness in public men at the expense both of fullness and exactness." So literary societies saved the educational experience from itself, at least in one opinion.

The societies were student organized and run with minimal faculty involvement. They took their college experience seriously and wanted to become men of character. Membership was selective, implying that dues might have been collected but at the very least there had to be evidence of commitment. As the financial situation worsened later in the decade, membership waned.

The Polytechnic men did not wait to organize. During the very first month of classes in 1891, the Philosophian Literary Society formed. Every Monday morning, the Philosophians met and presented the prepared part of their program. The idea was for each student to cultivate confidence and self-control before an audience. Then a debate topic would be thrown out to encourage quick thinking and expression.

The root word of their name, "philosopher" comes from the Greek meaning "lover of wisdom." Even their motto was high brow: *"Eloquence clothes man with kingly powers."*

They also picked colors. To the nineteenth century educated person, colors carried the weight of symbolism. The German philosopher, Johann Wolfgang von Goethe, developed a theory which remarkably touched on the psychology of color and how color affects us, so color theory was in the air. The young men picked white and pink. On Goethe's color wheel, red is a pure color, a primary color not mixed with any other pigment, and it "conveys an impression of gravity and dignity, and at the same time of grace and attractiveness…thus the dignity of age and the amiableness of youth may adorn itself with degrees of the same hue."[1] Because the men picked pink, it suggests they aspired to the dignity of red but were aware a process was required to achieve it. White is associated with purity, but psychologists tell us white also aids in mental clarity.

All this contributes to the goals and character of the Philosophian man. A description included in the early *Polytechnic Catalogue* stated their purpose this way: "Through the guidance of the society, the Philosophians, who viewed themselves as lovers of wisdom, learned that wisdom comes gradually by persistent work and conquest."

The very next semester of the first school year, another literary society formed (thanks in part to J. W. Adkisson's encouragement), specifically designed to create a competitive atmosphere. Quickly popular, the membership numbers equaled the Philosophians. Dubbed the Philamantheon Literary Society, the root word was Greek for "lover of learning." The similarities in the two names apparently caused confusion so the Philamantheons changed theirs a couple of years later to the Adkissonians. They met at the same time, at 9 am on Monday morning, and used the same format of prepared presentation and debates, but the similarities ended there.

A distinctive character began to define the two societies. From the beginning, the Adkissonians apparently felt the need to prove themselves to the Philosophians. They took pride in being the type of men who hearkened back to "the hardy pioneers who braved the wilderness in America. They were high-minded, sturdy, strenuous and resourceful... scholarship par excellence, pure athletics, manhood sublime."[2] In other words, a salt-of-the-earth kind of man.

The guys who were Adkissonians did not get picked in the first round whether because of a lack of privilege, of cultural experiences, or previous education. These were the scrappers, the farm boys, the athletes who believed that a college education had the power to change their lives. "Lover of learning" indeed.

With this in mind, their motto may have had a bit of a jab in it. "Brevity is the soul of wit." Perhaps a lack of vocabulary could be an advantage against a windbag full of words. Their color also carried meaning: sky blue, as if the sky is the limit. Going back to Goethe's color theory: "We readily follow an agreeable object that flies from us, so we love to contemplate blue—not because it advances to us but because it draws us after it." In addition they picked a flower, the white rose. Then, as now, the rose means love.

To build drama around the societies, a contest was held every year and awards were given. The first year of the contest, an Adkissonian won the Oratorical category and a Philosophian won the Debate, proving they could hold their own.

While the friendly rivalry was certainly a part of the literary society life, they could also cooperate with one another. They joined forces with the women's society to publish a monthly student newspaper called *The Polytechnian*. Later, as the financial situation stabilized, they began publishing a yearbook in 1906 and attempts were made to publish a newspaper weekly instead of monthly. They established and maintained libraries that at one point had more volumes than the college library.

Perhaps the biggest benefit of the literary societies was to keep everyone on their toes.

Susan M. Keys Literary Society
Courtesy, Texas Wesleyan University Special Collections.

EIGHTEEN

THE SUSAN M. KEYS: WOMEN'S LITERARY SOCIETY

Early on, the women's literary society was organized and well thought-out. In fact, it seemed to get an earlier start than the men's. For one thing, the group was named for a woman who died before the school year even began, evidence that students, faculty, and administration knew each other well in their efforts to get Polytechnic off the ground.

Susan Key, known as Susie to her friends and family, was Joseph Key's first wife. As Bishop, his vision led to a more multifaceted college in North Texas that would become Polytechnic. Born in Georgia, married at a young age and with three children, Susie apparently wielded influence of her own that doesn't come through in her obituary. This description found its way into the pledge ceremony, obviously written by someone who knew her.

> "Years ago a dear little woman endeared herself to the hearts of students through her exquisite life. She was a beautiful person in body and her brilliant intelligence shone out through shining eyes; she was gracious in manner; and was blessed for she knew God. This wonderful person was Susan M. Key, wife of Bishop Key. Because she was noble and lived to serve, a group of girls took her life as a pattern, and named themselves *The Susan M. Keys*."

While the men were content with learning to debate, the Keys' mission was to "help mold the character of the girls and prepare them physically, mentally, socially and spiritually for the future." That was how they described the four-fold life they aspired to and Key members were seekers.

The women loved their symbolism. Like the men with their colors and a motto, the Keys used gold for their color and the daisy for their flower. Their motto was interesting: "Victory crowns labor."

In Greek, 'stephanos' is the word for victor's crown and appears in New Testament Greek dictionaries and concordances. So the victor's crown was a common image. One definition in the NAS New Testament Greek lexicon is the metaphorical one: "the eternal blessedness which will be given as a prize to the genuine servants of God and Christ, the crown (wreath) which is the reward of the righteousness." But what must one do to get crowned? Labor. This is also an interesting choice.

The end of the nineteenth century was a time of change for society but especially for women. There was the concept of the separate spheres for men and women, the realm of women being the home. Within the home, women were encouraged to become educated so they were better prepared to raise children to be thinking and productive citizens.

With the rise of an industrial financial base, more women and children were working outside of the home. Because conditions were so bad, they began to organize for better working conditions. With education comes possibility and optimism, both within and outside of the scope of 'homebody.' So the word 'labor' in their motto has connotations that these women were embracing in their new role with enthusiasm.

The Keys also set up an elaborate ceremony filled with symbolism. During the initiation, a candle was lit for each fold, represented by a door. They *were* Keys, after all.

The Four Folds:

"1. *Physical Fitness*—we would have you be physically strong and beautiful. And would remember that your bodies are temples for the Devine [sic], we would have you reverence them.

2. *Mental Alertness*—Because we are made with growing intellects we would keep our minds open to all the wealth of knowledge that surrounds us, and improve 'each shining moment.'

3. *Social Poise*—There is no greater art than that of living happily with people. We want to live so well in daily contact with our fellows that we will excel in social graces.

4. *Spiritual Beauty*—this devine [sic] spark that dwells within each one of us is the thing that makes us akin to God. We want to pause in the tasks of life to hear a still small voice 'which will guide us to Eternity.'"

The initiation continued. The doors of life could be opened with a golden key set with thirteen pearls. Pearls were a symbol of purity and members were told that each pearl also stood for a virtue of womanhood: love, honor, sincerity, understanding, courage, self-control, loyalty, gratitude, humility, faith, purity, hope, and justice.

Given all the negative feelings about thirteen, it is startling that the golden key of the Keys has thirteen pearls. Pearls themselves are a symbol of purity, in keeping with the ideal for women. But thirteen? Why not an even dozen?

Analysis does not reveal obvious answers. Within the Christian faith, thirteen has all kinds of negative associations. There were thirteen at the Last Supper once Judas finally arrived after arranging his betrayal of Jesus. Tradition has Good Friday occurring on the 13th. On Friday the 13th in the year 1307, hits were carried out on the Knights Templar and the Pope wiped out the entire order in one day. That's a lot of negativity.

So why was thirteen part of the Keys' symbolism?

There are a few positive associations. In medieval theology, the number thirteen was a memory device to help the serfs remember the important part of their faith: Ten Commandments plus the Holy Trinity—ten plus three equals thirteen. In ancient Greece, Zeus was considered the thirteenth god, large and in charge. Connected to Zeus, thirteen represented totality, completion, power, realization, and attainment. With both these systems, completion is a strong aspect.

Thirteen is a prime number and the only number that is prime when the digits are switched (thirty-one). Primes tend to carry a meaning of incorruptible nature, purity, and integrity.

What is also intriguing (but unclear if it was in the women's minds) is the divine feminine significance of the number thirteen. Before Christianity hit the scene, for those female-centric belief systems, thirteen was a sacred number. There are thirteen lunar cycles and thirteen menstrual cycles. When the Catholic Church usurped those pagan cultures, they turned thirteen into a "bad" number and made witches evil and in league with the devil to break their hold on their communities.

Did any of this survive to become part of the Keys' symbolism? That's complete speculation. These young women were feisty, but maybe not to a conscious extent such as that.

NINETEEN

PROFILE: MARVIN COPPEDGE & ADA BROOKS

Another promising minister to come out of Polytechnic was Marvin Coppedge, class of 1895, but he was cut down in his youth.

Marvin was valedictorian of his class. At the commencement ceremony held in the college chapel, he read his essay titled "Service of Humanity." Even at this point, he had been licensed to preach for six years. His Methodist memoir says "He felt that a call to preach was also a call to get ready to preach so he devoted himself with great earnestness to obtaining an education."

He taught for a year at Polytechnic, but Marvin may have had other motives than giving back to his alma mater. His eye had caught that of another student: Ada Brooks. The year of 1895-96 may have been about wooing her, too.

At any rate, they married in 1896 and Marvin Jr. was born in 1897. By then Marvin Sr. was on the pastor circuit in East Texas. Two years later, he was assigned to the Oklahoma Conference. His brother Charles M. Coppedge was a leader ministering to the Native American tribes there, so that may have played a part in Marvin and Ada and little Marvin going to Checotah where the Creek nation was located.

On June 1, 1899, Marvin, Ada, and Junior headed home to visit the family, but he never left his father's house. He died on June 14, cause of death unreported. But there are some clues as to what might have happened.

In 1899, there were several outbreaks of some nasty diseases; reports included measles, meningitis, flu (not the Spanish flu, that would be 1918), and pneumonia. But most troubling was a bad smallpox epidemic in Texas. It was thought to be spread by workers along the railroad lines, with cases coming up from Mexico and in Oklahoma among the Native Americans, including the Creeks.

Although naturally occurring, there is no cure for the disease. Smallpox was wiped out by 1980 and eradicated because of a commitment to vaccinations.

Symptoms of the disease do not appear until a person has been infected for ten to fourteen days. Then suddenly the victims seems to have the flu with fever, achiness, headache, listlessness, back pain. A few days later, red spots appear usually on face, hands, and forearms then follow on the chest and back. These spots turn into blisters, first filled with clear liquid then pus. Scabs form eight to ten days later and when they fall off, there are the deep, tell-tale scars. There can even be sores in the nose and mouth.

How is smallpox spread?

Of course, face to face contact would do it. Anyone who visited an infected person could be at risk, usually through exposure to droplets in the air when the sufferer coughs, sneezes, or talks. Items such as bedding or clothing could become contaminated, so just doing an infected patient's laundry would carry a risk. In the 1890s, smallpox sufferers would be quarantined. If there were many cases, a separate house or "pest" house would be set up to contain the outbreak.

So how does that relate to Marvin?

In April, Polytechnic was closed because of a case of smallpox. Patient zero was a young man named Russell Brooks. It is not clear how close a relation he was to Ada, but they were from the same small town. Nevertheless, their lives were intertwined. They had all been at Polytechnic at the same time and they knew each other. Russell appears to have survived his smallpox because records show he took over Marvin's church in Checotah after he died.

About two years later, Ada married Marvin's brother, Harvey, and they settled in Dallas.

SMALLPOX
KEEP OUT OF THIS HOUSE
By Order of BOARD OF HEALTH

HEALTH OFFICER

Any person removing this card without authority is liable to prosecution.

TWENTY

EAST SIDE OF TOWN: POLYTECHNIC HEIGHTS

The Hall and Tandy influence on the east side of Fort Worth is everywhere. Because Lewis Tandy (class of aught four) became a real estate guy, the Tandy name lives on as a street, as businesses in the Meadowbrook neighborhood, and even in the Tandy Hills Nature Reserve. The Halls, though less flashy, were no less part of the landscape. They also played a major role in the process of turning prairie into a civilized town.

As soon as the Texas and Pacific Railroad Company solved the problem of bridging Sycamore Creek, more settlers arrived and the east side began to develop. With those settlers came the need for basic services like a school, a church, a trading post, and a blacksmith. As people worked together, they naturally organized into a town. The school built near Arch Hall's house was for any neighboring children whose parents saw fit to send them, whether tenants or landholders. In 1886, a Vassar graduate was hired to teach them.

Roger Tandy dammed a portion of the creek to make Tandy Lake. It became famous for hunting, fishing, picnics, and dances. In fact, William Tandy, Roger's brother, was called "the county's famous turkey hunter." According to the *Texas Breeding Bird Atlas*, turkeys were abundant in Texas.

Tandy Lake was quite the recreational spot into the early twentieth century, so it seemed a logical place for a town as well. Eventually there would be a train stop at Tandy Lake when the interurban ran from Fort Worth to Dallas, in an area approximately located between today's Ayers and Collard streets.

The opening of Polytechnic College in 1891 can trace its literal roots to the land donation by Arch Hall, W. D. Hall, and Roger and George Tandy, Roger's son. With a college in the area, it was time to get serious about development. They were all savvy enough to realize cities need the financial security business brings. So they helped bring a cotton mill to the area.

The mill was dubbed Manchester Mills, usually attributed to Manchester, England, the hub of cotton weaving in England. Mike Nichols, local historian, points out that W. Z. Manchester was a local businessman and

Fourteen-year-old spinner in a Brazos Valley Cotton Mill in West, Texas.
Courtesy, Library of Congress.

The first grocery store in Polytechnic opened in 1892 by S.S. Dillow.
Courtesy, Texas Wesleyan University Special Collections (Dillow Collection).

entrepreneur who was very involved in the economic expansion of Fort Worth. His name comes up in the Fort Worth paper connected to business and real estate dealings. One article even talks about "Manchester, the factory addition to the west of Fort Worth" and there is still a neighborhood called Manchester Heights. But that's the west side and the cotton mill was on the east side. The point is that if Manchester was known so well and he was involved with a cotton mill, people would call it Manchester Mills.

Cotton mills were a part of the recovery of the South from the Civil War, but Texas was slow to catch the fever. When they did, the boom in mill building was driven mainly by the expansion of the railroad. The first was the Dallas Cotton Mills in 1888, followed by mills in Galveston and Corsicana in 1890, and Sherman Manufacturing in 1891. Manchester Mills was part of the phenomenon, opening in 1891.

One pioneer remembers Manchester Mills as a rambling two-story brick building right next to the tracks at what is now Ayres Road. With the mill a done deal, there would also be forty houses built around it. Typically, mill towns or villages would grow up alongside a mill. While that does not seem to be the case as much in Texas in 1890, there was housing construction thanks to the mill.

Cotton mills were high tech for their day. Machines everywhere had a specific job but the end game took raw cotton, separated, straightened and twisted cotton fibers, then made yarn and wove the yarn into cloth. There was a machine to take apart the cotton compressed in shipping and cleaning it of dirt and short fibers. A machine could only do so much. Humans finished the job and fed the cotton into carding machines. Workers fed this bit into a set of rollers to make the fibers thinner, then a machine twisted it. This twisted thread was wound on bobbins which had to be frequently changed out. Spoolers combined threads from ten to fifteen different bobbins and had to tie broken ends together.

Manchester Mill produced cloth, so it had a weave room with a set of large looms which had to be hand laced. The mill may have had thirty to fifty employees.

Certainly the mill housing and its workers added to the need for services on the east side as well as transportation, but the mill did not provide those services. The Halls and the Tandys financed the laying of tracks for a streetcar line to bring folks from town out to the mill and the college. Other businesses like grocers had a reason to come to the area and when the post office was installed, it was for the town of Manchester Mills.

There is no record of what the college students thought of the mill workers who might well have been their same age but in vastly different circumstances. Instead of writing essays, the young women worked around loud machinery, breathing in cotton fibers and dirt, pushing slivers of cotton into rollers or maintaining the width of thread on the spinners. Instead of discussing literary themes, the women might make cloth in the weave room, directing threads from a cone of freshly spun thread onto the beams of the loom. Even though the mill workers had a long workday, they would never be as well off as the young women who went to college. In fact, they might not have known how to read, but they worked hard and tried to be good to the people around them.

When the cotton mill burned in October of 1893, it's very likely Polytechnic students helped extinguish the fire. They were often called on to form bucket brigades and help put out fires in the neighborhood. Fires were common because buildings were wooden structures and gas lamps and steam driven boilers did not help matters.

By 1893, the college was a fixture. Some of its business majors might have hoped to get a management job at the mill but within hours of the fire, the mill was history. Fort Worth was in the depths of the Panic of 1893 so there was no money to rebuild. They simply moved on and all those mill workers were out of a job.

The neighborhood was known as Manchester Mills for another ten or so years. By then, Polytechnic College and Methodist Church looked like they were going to stay. Instead of buying homes and establishing businesses to serve the mill families, people moved to the neighborhood because they wanted their kids to go to school at Polytechnic, resulting in a boom for the area surrounding the college. In 1910, the post office officially became Polytechnic Heights and the name stuck. Some of the residents called it Methodist Hill or Poly Hill.

One family who relocated to Polytechnic for college was the Hunter family, according to family records. The Hunter parents served as dorm managers of the men's dorm. All four of the children were enrolled in either the preparatory school or the college. One son, Clement, contracted consumption (known today as tuberculosis). Clarence would become a pharmacist and later opened a pharmacy across the street from the college campus. Callie became a teacher, but she too contracted consumption.

When Clement died in his twenties, the family picked up and moved south to a warmer climate, but they left their mark on the neighborhood like many others would.

In 1922, the town of Polytechnic Heights was annexed by the city. Many Poly alumni were part of the often fierce debates, but it came down to the fact that Fort Worth could provide more city services than the little village could.

Still, residents would continue to identify themselves as being from Polytechnic Heights.

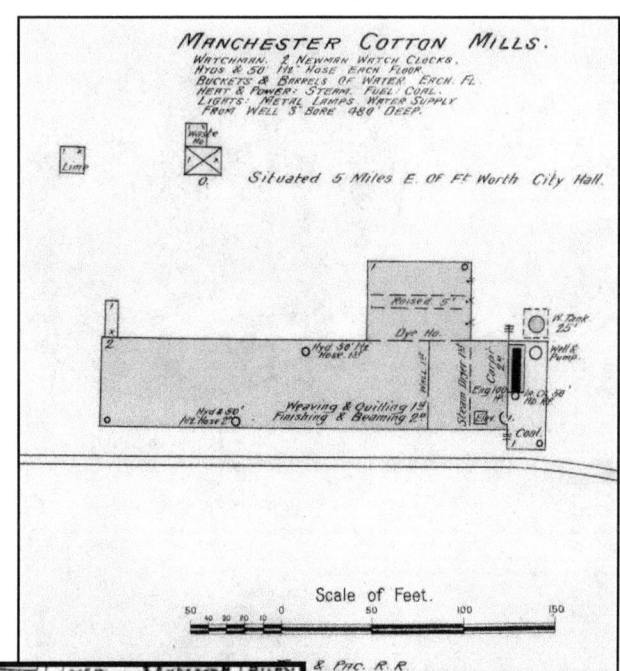

Sanborn map of Manchester Mills cotton mill.

Courtesy, Library of Congress

Antique street map showing the mill and the college.

Public Domain.

Noble Adkisson

Anna Kanouse Adkisson

Photos from Kanouse Family Portrait, c. 1908. Courtesy, Kent Kanouse.

TWENTY-ONE
PROFILE: NOBLE ADKISSON AND ANNA KANOUSE

So much fuss was made about keeping male and female students separated at Polytechnic, how big a scandal was it for an instructor to marry a student? Eyebrows raised. Whispers behind their back.

One such instructor was Noble Adkisson, so maybe allowances were made for an Adkisson. He was young, only twenty-five. He had impressive credentials: degrees from University of Louisville and Vanderbilt. He wrote a play that was published and frequently performed, a strongly anti-alcohol and surprisingly abolitionist play called "Ruined by Drink." Teaching at Polytechnic was Noble's first job.

The student in question was Anna Kanouse, a young woman from Bowie, Texas, and she was part of Polytechnic's first class. Her father was a successful businessman. She must have lived on campus, so she would have known Annie Adkisson before she died. Anna Kanouse was vice president of the Epworth League that year.

How would Noble have courted Anna? How did they come to the decision to marry? Did they face the disapproval of families? There is no record of how all of this happened. They married between semesters in January 1893. Anna continued to take piano and guitar lessons at Polytechnic but did not complete a degree. If students wanted to take classes without pursuing a degree, they were allowed to do so.

Noble and Anna seemed to be quite the vagabonds for the next few years. Noble taught a year at Granbury College, two years at Randolph College, and two years at Terrell University School. Then they moved to Denton and Noble was on the first faculty of an all-women school called College of Industrial Arts, which would later become Texas Women's College. He taught Physical Science, which included Physics and Chemistry. He found a home at this college and stayed until he retired. Almost twenty years later, a new item appears in the San Marcos newspaper: "It is said that the laboratory in physics at the College [of Industrial Arts], which has been developed under the immediately [sic] direction of Professor Adkisson, is one of the best in the Southwest."

Noble is credited with taking one of the earliest surviving photographs of the campus; he was pursuing his artistic interests along with his professional ones.

Anna also seemed to find her home in Denton. She was involved at the First Methodist Church, especially in the Women's Missionary Society. A founding member of the Shakespeare Club, she participated in its activities for fifty years. She was the first woman to ever serve on the public school board and did so for twelve years. In 1956, the Denton Junior Chamber of Commerce honored her with the Woman of the Year award.

Anna was well-known for her kindness, cultivating connections that endeared her to many. When someone appeared in the newspaper, she clipped the article and mailed it to the subject with a handwritten note, often congratulating or encouraging the news-maker. The paper staff at one point tried to reimburse her for the postage. Anna insisted that the clipping gave her so much joy that was payment enough.

Noble and Anna led lives of quiet kindness and excellence, so perhaps there was no scandal at all when they married.

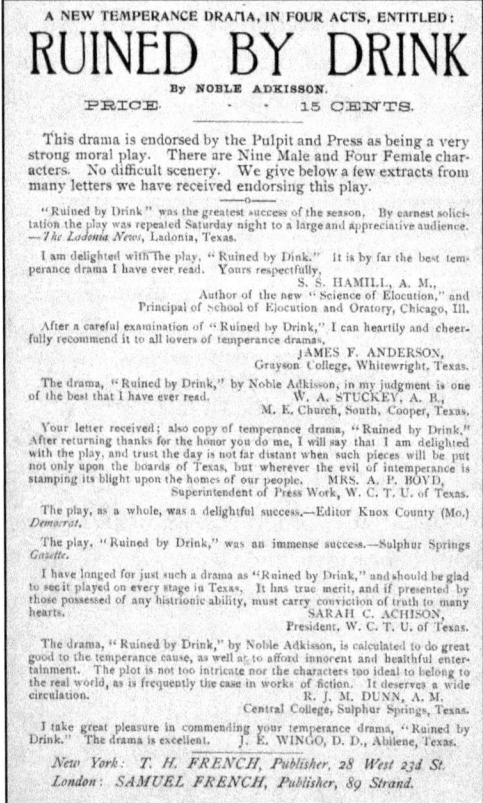

Ad for Noble Adkisson's Play

Courtesy, Texas Wesleyan Special Collections.

TWENTY-TWO

TROUBLEMAKERS AND PRANKSTERS

According to Richard Johnston's family lore, his grandfather Scott Johnston sneaked out of the dorm—and he was not the only one. The young men were fascinated with the street car parked at the end of the Polytechnic line at night. Scott jumped into the driver's seat and figured out how to start the car. Unfortunately, he could not suss out how to stop it and could only crash. The punishment, if any, failed to survive with the rest of the story.

The subject of discipline was not addressed in the college catalogues until 1895, and even then in rather mild terms. As C. L. Browning said of the first class, "It was a good group of boys and girls." As the enrollment increased, a need must have arisen to set some ground rules.

The policy was vague. "The discipline of the college is mild, but firm. Every infraction of the rules, if known, will be visited by a suitable penalty." This would give the faculty room to be as strict or as lenient as each circumstance allowed. It also revealed how much faith they had in the integrity of their students.

Still, kids will be kids.

Leon Sensabaugh said he and others sneaked out to see the renowned actor Walker Whiteside in a Shakespearean play. In order to do so, they had to go to their rooms, report (essentially lie) to the room monitor, turn off their lights, lock their doors, and climb out the window. They still had a long walk to catch the streetcar and hope no one saw them.

Says Leon: "Those were heroic days and only the most daring souls could see the great outside except under supervision. But with all that it was a mighty decent bunch of boys and girls who attended school in those days."

John Creed tells of a particularly unsportsmanlike prank after a fierce debate competition. The rivalry between the Philosophians and the Adkissonians had become heated. John didn't set up the story with what caused the especially bad blood that year. The Philosophians came out on top in the competition, and they were not content with just winning. They had to rub it in the Adkissonians' face. Between midnight and day-break, a figure was fashioned out of straw and buried in a little grave on campus, marked with a tombstone that said, "Little Add." In addition, there was a poetic epitaph attached.

The Adkissonians were furious to be teased along with their defeat. Apparently the insulting grave was discovered early that morning. A crowd gathered and "civil war broke out." John does not elaborate beyond that, particularly whether fisticuffs were part of the conflict, but the faculty had to intervene.

Punishment would have been swift and severe, except the Philosophian pranksters timed it well. Everyone left for the break that day and the perpetrators' identities remain a mystery.

The board of trustees recorded in their minutes the need for a discipline policy in 1896 because they had to "resort to severe discipline in only two cases." The actual list of demerits did not appear until 1900. Once a student accumulated 30 demerits, they were expelled. There is no record of anyone actually being sent home so perhaps the threat was enough. Some of the offenses seem minor, while some are serious enough infractions they deserve the full weight of the law.

- Absent from recitations without excuse-2
- Failure to prepare recitation without excuse-2
- Failure to prepare composition-5
- Failure to prepare term essay or oration-10
- Failure to stand examination-15
- Receiving or giving aid in examination-30
- Leaving recitation without excuse-2
- Disorder in recitation-3
- Absent from Church or Sabbath School without excuse-3
- Absent from Chapel without excuse-3
- Indecorous conduct in public worship-5
- Tardiness in any class duties-1
- Smoking publicly-5
- Drinking spirituous liquors or gambling-30
- Claiming to have quit school as a pretext for violating rules-30
- Assuming suspension privileges without permission-5
- Loitering around stores and forbidden place during study hours-5
- Absent from rooms at night-15
- Leaving College Hill and premises without permission-5
- Neglect of music practice-5
- Entering into combination to interrupt and hinder or thwart College order and discipline-30
- Any and all other violations of order, not herein specified-2 to 30

When a student reached ten, he was warned; twenty, he would receive a second warning and parent notification; thirty and he was out. These rules were so important they were in two places in the 1901 *Bulletin*.

But some of these rules! The one about "indecorous conduct in public worship" raises questions about what did "indecorous" actually entail. Laughing? Sleeping? It carried a rather hefty penalty of five points. It would be better to be absent (three points) than to be "indecorous." Smoking carried the same penalty as "indecorous."

If a student pretended to quit, he may as well have gone ahead since it got him thirty points. Being a rabble-rouser and encouraging others to break the rules got him the boot. Obviously cheating and drinking and gambling would get a person expelled. If Leon had been caught, the cumulative effect could have been severe. But then his father was a trustee at the time.

Beware especially the handy-dandy catch-all:

"Any and all other violations of order herein not specified."

Oratory Contestants
Courtesy, Texas Wesleyan Special Collections.

Strawman, facing page: Courtesy, Vector Me.

Front Cover of First Crisco Cookbook: Public Domain.
Facing page: Leon Sensabaugh photo courtesy, Southern Methodist University Archives.

TWENTY-THREE

PROFILE: LEON SENSABAUGH

Leon was not sure what he was going to do with his life, but he wasn't going to preach. At Polytechnic he went the business route and earned a degree in bookkeeping. Perhaps a surprising choice for the son of a dynamic and pioneering Methodist minister but at the end of his career, Leon said he was "called to teach, not to preach."

Before the teaching part, Leon was a fun-loving kid. His father, O. F. Sensabaugh, was touted as the first Methodist preacher west of the Continental Divide. Leon spent much of his young life in New Mexico and Colorado. His mother died when he was quite young and his father married Daisy Lane, a graduate of the new Southwestern College in Georgetown, Texas, who was a teacher at the Ramona Indian School in Santa Fe. Even early, Leon's life was full of adventure.

At Polytechnic, Leon sneaked out of the dorm after curfew on a regular basis. He claimed to have a different girlfriend every year he was at Polytechnic. In those early days, the school attempted to keep the boys and girls separated or at least under the watchful eye of faculty. Leon revealed that play practice was a lot more than learning lines!

On a more serious note, he was involved with the Philomathians, so much so that he took credit for helping usher in the new name of Adkissonians. He won oratory contests and debates, graduating in 1898. But he did not want to preach.

It is not clear what he did for the next few years but around 1902, he ended up in Dublin, Texas. He married Effie Frank from Stephenville. She attended Tarleton and the St. Louis Music Conservatory. Her hometown paper called her "the most talented pianist in the state." Eventually her father ran for county judge in Stephenville.

First Leon ran a farm, then he ran for county clerk. He sold real estate then he ran for tax assessor/collector. Each time he ran for office, he backed out because some business opportunity dropped in his lap. For a while he was the manager of the Dublin Cotton Oil Company.

Never heard of cotton oil? Yes, you have, but maybe by another name: *Crisco*.

Cotton was a huge cash crop for the South, and Texas in particular. Many a Texas town's economy was based on cotton. Everyone knows about the fiber, but cotton plants produce more pounds of seed than fiber. For generations this seed was garbage, rotting into toxic waste.

As early as the 1820s, folks experimented with finding a use for the seeds. By the 1850s, some bright person was able to get oil from them and it was used for gas lamps. When crude oil was discovered, the demand for cottonseed oil disappeared.

Then someone said, "Let's cook with it!" Proctor and Gamble discovered a chemical process that turned cottonseed oil into a solid fat like lard. Unfortunately, this also transformed it into 'trans' fat. Without knowing any better, they marketed this new lard-like substance as a food. It made pastry flakier! Fried food crisper! Didn't go rancid!

Crisco became the miracle product for the new century. Easier to digest (they said)! Cheaper than lard! Now we know better, but Texas farmers and businessmen saw a way to survive. With Leon's experience as a farmer and a degree in business, Dublin Oil Company was glad to have him.

Yet it still was not the right fit. Leon began liquidating his business interests and moved his family. First to Fort Worth to sell furniture, then to San Diego, California. There is no clear reason for his restlessness but Effie and their two sons were no reason to stay put. Leon was headed west again.

What was a constant in his life at this point was his passionate involvement with the Epworth League. Perhaps it started at Polytechnic.

In the 1890s, the Epworth League was a young organization that eventually became Methodist Youth Fellowship. A familiar name appears in the annual of the Epworth League: Bishop Joseph Key established it in North Texas. There was an Epworth League at Polytechnic almost before the literary societies could get a foothold and provided students with a social group.

Leagues popped up all over Texas. Their purpose was to "develop young church members in their religious life and to provide training in churchmanship." Statewide membership swelled to 10,000 by 1896, the state organization publishing a paper and establishing a camp in Corpus Christi called Epworth-by-the-Sea in 1905. Epworth League conventions were remarkably integrated with Blacks, Indians, Asians, and Hispanics attending.

Leon was in the thick of it, serving on the regional committee every year despite business dealings and family responsibilities.

By the time Leon registered for the draft in 1918, he had embraced his calling. His place of employment was Trinity Methodist in Los Angeles and his job was Director of Religious Studies. He spelled everything out in spite of the small box on the form, as if determined to forge a path where there was none.

He earned a doctorate from Vanderbilt, published books about Sunday School that became training manuals, and organized youth camps. He spoke at conventions on topics like "How To Have Fun," hearkening back to his Polytechnic days. In 1933, he landed at Highland Park Methodist in Dallas. He divided his time between establishing a program of Christian education at the church and holding special programs for Southern Methodist college students. His leadership was lauded for using the latest trends to up the game for training students so they might become ethical citizens with a moral base. It was as if he channeled the fundamentals on which Polytechnic was founded in a new way, the precursor to Vacation Bible School, youth camps, and youth groups of today's churches. His efforts have also inspired others who wanted to do church work but were "called to teach, not to preach."

The fun-loving kid at Polytechnic built a career around the notion that "recreation and fellowship were as important as Bible study and worship in developing a well-rounded Christian life."

The spirit seemed to inspire his daughter, Ludi Mae. His two sons became academics; George was recognized for how he mentored students. Ludi Mae, the precocious baby of the family, loved music and theatre. She organized Dallas Children's Theatre among her many projects in the local theatre scene. In the 1930s, she had a radio program that aired on Sunday nights and its main sponsor was Dr. Pepper, another Dublin original. The name of her show was *Miss Sugah and Her Boy Friends*.

Ludi Mae Sensabaugh seated between Jimmie Jeffries (left) and Joe Reichman (right), a local pianist and orchestra leader. c. 1937
From the collections of the Dallas History & Archives Division, Dallas Public Library

Class of 1898
(left to right)
Lilly Oswalt, Collin Perry, J. Fred Newsom,
L.F. Sensabaugh, Ella Ray, Hattie Keller
Courtesy, Southern Methodist University Archives.

TWENTY-FOUR

PROFILE: GEORGE SENSABAUGH

Leon's younger brother, George, was at Polytechnic in 1898, the year Leon graduated. He even began the 1899 school year. For some reason, he did not go back for the spring semester. In January 1900, George enlisted in the Army even though he would not turn eighteen until February. Why was he so anxious to go to war?

Sensational journalism had whipped American sympathy for Cuba and other Spanish colonies as reports of Spain's brutal handling of the Cuban rebellion for independence surfaced. Even if George had been influenced by this reporting, the war in Cuba was over in 1898, thanks to American intervention.

However, tensions in the Philippines continued. Now that Spain had been painted as the Big Bad Wolf in the world, perhaps George was compelled to enlist. A treaty and a buy-out had already been reached between the U. S. and Spain. It was just that the Philippines did not want to replace one dictator with another foreign invader (America). Once Spain withdrew, the Filipinos turned on the U. S. soldiers. The war drug on for three long years. Body count: 4,200 Americans; 20,000 Filipino soldiers; 200,000 Filipino civilians.

Reading news accounts of the day in November 1899, the Filipinos resisted the "kindly" efforts of the United States to take over peacefully. Emilio Aguinaldo had been leading efforts to keep America out of their country, but he realized they could not win a conventional war. So they shifted to guerrilla-style warfare. President McKinley kept fanning the pro-war flames in order to entice the American public to stay the course in the Philippines. The entire time George was in the Philippines, he faced a brutal war that included killing civilians and burning villages, torture on both sides of the conflict, disease, and food shortages.

George came from a family of missionaries. Service was in his DNA and the call he heard in the night was to help the people of the Philippines.

The reality was far different. Here's what J. E. Fetterly, a soldier from Nebraska, said: "Some think the insurgents are disheartened, but I think they will make a desperate struggle for what they consider their rights. I do not approve of the course our government is pursuing with these people.

If all men are created equal, they have some rights which ought to be respected."

In official papers to the war department, the causes of death were specific. Some men died in combat, some by cholera, malaria, and dysentery. Then there was the term "killed by comrade." That was how George died. Friendly fire. The local paper reported that he was in the province of Samar which is where the heaviest action was and he was shot while scouting. His body was shipped home from Calbayog City.

George Sensabaugh was 5 feet 7 inches, dark brown hair, fair complexion. He was nineteen years old.

He never graduated from Polytechnic.

U.S. troops in action during Philippine-American War 1899
Public Domain

TWENTY-FIVE
DEGREE PLANS

At first, Polytechnic wanted to offer everything. Music, business, literature, classical, practical. Finally, organizers had to face the fact they could not offer every degree and stay afloat. Something had to go. In 1899, administrators decided they could not adequately prepare a Master's level student. So they discontinued that program and focused on their Bachelor's degree plans for Arts, Literature, and Science.

In addition to Bachelor's and Master's degrees, the college awarded a certificate for some subjects, most of them business. Students could earn certificates in bookkeeping, stenography, shorthand, business, elocution, and music. While they were listed as graduates, they did not seem to have the same prestige that degreed students had.

Then there was something called an *amanuensis certificate*.

According to WiseGeek.com, an amanuensis (pronounced ah-MANU-wen-sihs) is a person who writes things by hand by taking dictation, recopying or working somehow with the written word. At the time, someone with an amanuensis certificate could work as a personal assistant, scribe for a business or service that dealt with people who were illiterate, or for a railroad or shipping company. The more highly educated and multi-lingual this person was, the more valuable he or she was to an employer.

Polytechnic had a growing preparatory school called "sub-freshman." They were able to add a primary program by 1895. Class placement in either the college level program or the preparatory school was dependent on how well the prospective student did on their entrance exams, not their age. As soon as the student mastered the material, he or she could move up. In fact, Polytechnic Preparatory School was touted over other prep schools because the students had access to a large library and participation in the literary societies. But college and sub-freshmen alike could live in the boarding facilities.

By the middle of the decade, the music department divided itself into schools. Concentrations included voice, piano, violin, and guitar with a chorus and orchestra as performing opportunities. Many had to perform recitals as well as offer their talents to literary society and church programs.

The School of Commerce offered abbreviated programs in business skills and compared favorably with any of the country's business colleges.

Classes offered included bookkeeping, arithmetic, commercial law, and business correspondence, all rather self-explanatory.

But one class seems a bit mysterious as to why a business person would need it: "Rapid Calculation." Through class exercises, students practiced all kinds of math with the goal of doing these calculations quickly, including fractions and interest. According to the college catalog, "These practice drills are of great benefit in developing speed and self-reliance."

The advantage of studying business at Polytechnic over a business school, the catalogue was quick to point out, was the Christian environment and being around students of great character. The campus was far away from gambling *hells* (not sure if that was intentional or a typographical error), whiskey saloons, or other dangerous places. For the business classes, tuition was charged by the course.

If any of the literary students wanted to take a business course, they could add it for a discounted tuition.

Before distance learning was cool, Polytechnic had a correspondence school. Students who took advantage of this arrangement were like modern-day distance learners. Perhaps they had a job they could not leave or did not have a way to leave their life at home, but they could still obtain an education. Lessons were mailed back and forth, students having the benefit of trained instructors and regular assignments. These could be applied toward a degree plan and graduation.

The correspondence classes were tailored for preachers and teachers, and the tuition rate was low: ten dollars for each class.

What a bargain!

Polytechnic College Alumni
1891-1901

C. L. Browning, A.M.

Marvin Coppedge, A.B., A.M.

Florence Henderson, M.E.L.

Beaulah Thompson, M.E.L.

Bessie Baker, A.B.

Eva Hall, B.S. & Music

Ladye Dennis, M.E.L.

T. L. Rippey, B.S.

Dora Walkup, Music

John Hall, Music

Marion Bailey, Business

John R. Blanton, Business

E.G. Stovey, Business

Lizzie Collins, Business

J. F. Newsom, B.S.

S. R. Wright, Business

Mary Elizabeth "Lizzie" Adkisson, M.E.L.

David Harris, Business

N. B. Turner, Business

Innie Kidd, M.E.L.

J. F. Potts, Business

Hugh Bard, Business

1896	1897
E. L. Spurlock, A.B.	J. H. Newton, B.S.
C. P. Hudson, B.S.	Clara Rogers, Elocution
Fannie Gulledge, M.E.L.	Florence Henderson, Elocution
Mabel Johnson, M.E.L.	Pearl Kennedy, Elocution
Beall Sawyer, M.E.L.	Gertrude Boone, Music
Lalla Duke, Bookkeeping	George Renie, Bookkeeping
Hines Mitchell, Bookkeeping	C. E. Hunter, Bookkeeping
	E. Appleyard, Bookkeeping
	A. V. Cocke, Bookkeeping
	J. T. Owen, Bookkeeping
	T. C. Daggett, Bookkeeping
	E. Sherwood, Bookkeeping
	A. A. Callaham, Bookkeeping
	L. O. West, Bookkeeping
	J. W. Martin, Bookkeeping
	Eula Jeans, Stenography

 **1898**

L. F. Sensabaugh, B.S.

J. F. Newsom, A.B.

Hattie Keller, M.E.L.

Ella Ray, M.E.L.

Lily Oswalt, M.E.L.

W. B. Duncan, A.B.

Lorena Collingsworth Perry, M.E.L.

Marguerite Dunn, Elocution

Dora Walkup, Elocution

Evangeline Brewer, Elocution

Lizzie Isaacs, Elocution

Mamie Richerson, Elocution

Ida Newsom, Elocution

Annie Vinson, Elocution

D.B. Singletary, Bookkeeping

 **1899**

No graduation took place this year due to smallpox case and campus closure.

1900

John W. Bagby, B.S.

John J. Creed, B.L.

Nannie Lou Grace, A.B. & Elocution

Charles Morton, B.L.

Annie Owen, A.B.

Nola Brown, M.E.L. & Elocution

Thomas Davis, A.B.

Stuart Lloyd, A.B.

Charles Owen, A.B.

Antone Laport Thomas, B.L.

Forest Uhl, A.B.

T. V. Ellzey, Elocution

Addison Rogers, Business

Otto Estes, Shorthand

Buford Brown, Shorthand

1901

John J. Creed, A.B.

E. C. Hunter, A.B.

J. E. Strong, Amanuensis

J. P. Parks, Amanuensis

E. F. Kimbrough, Amanuensis

Rosa Hardin, Amanuensis

Eula Jeanes, Amanuensis

W. T. Medley, Bookkeeping

W. E. Nicholson, Bookkeeping

P. N. Ingraham, Bookkeeping

TWENTY-SIX

PROFILE: ELLA RAY LEDGERWOOD

Ella Ray was a small town girl but she must have had big dreams. The daughter of a prominent Methodist minister, she spent her formative years in Dublin, Texas. Going to Polytechnic may have been an obvious choice since ministers' kids could go tuition free. But was it a good fit?

Ella kept a low profile. She did not sing or take piano lessons. No elocution classes for this girl. Yet as soon as she graduated, she was hired to teach art.

Lula Rippey, Lee Rippey's (class of 1893) sister, had been the first art professor at Polytechnic and was there in 1895 so she might have wielded some influence. When Lula appeared in later Polytechnic Catalogues, she had the credential of 'a student of Chase and Douthit, New York.'

New York City had already emerged as an artistic hub by the late nineteenth century. Any artist who wanted to make a name for themselves, especially in America, had to go to New York. It was the next best thing to going to Paris. Hudson Valley, in upstate New York, acquired its own reputation as a style, but even then those artists relied on New York City for galleries and patrons.

What did it mean that Lula was a student of Chase? William Merritt Chase, as an artist, was seeking his own style like other American artists of the day, borrowing from old masters and contemporary artists in an attempt to find his own uniqueness. As a teacher, he was esteemed at the Art Students League, traveling extensively in Europe and becoming acquainted with the major art figures of the day. His teaching methods must have reflected the highest standards. It opened in 1878 and was going strong by the mid-1890s, when Lula would have been there.

In this period he also ran a school at Shinnecock in the summers. It was an elegant town and a prestigious school which would have dazzled Lula, a Methodist minister's daughter from Texas. By the time she returned to Polytechnic in 1901, she must have had an air and a painting style that would have impressed or possibly intimidated Ella, the woman who stayed behind in Fort Worth to teach.

When Ella had been a student at Polytechnic, the art teacher was Mattie Melton, a privileged, provincial woman who was the daughter of a minor

Fort Worth mover and shaker, Colonel Jesse Melton. The *Fort Worth Gazette* frequently published news of "little Miss Mattie" and her travels. It seems unlikely she inspired Ella artistically although perhaps her willingness to travel opened some possibilities for the Dubliner.

Ella taught during the tumultuous year of 1899 when the school closed because of a smallpox breakout, the last of several calamities to hit the fledgling college. Would the college survive? What were her options? Maybe the time was right for her turn in New York City. At any rate, Lula was the art professor on record in 1901 with Ella back the following year of 1902.

Ella's artist biography listed her as a student of Irving Wiles and K. H. Miller in New York, both teachers at the Art Students League, William Chase's school. Lula and Ella's educational paths may have crossed in Texas, and their artists' paths met at the Art Students League, which would close in 1911.

Once Ella came back home to Fort Worth and settled into teaching and painting, she met a local attorney, Harry Ledgerwood from Michigan. They married in 1905. Ella remained in the *Polytechnic Catalogue* as the art professor for the 1905-06 school year, even renting out space for a studio in the same building where his offices were. The following year, her studio is listed as their home address. They had a baby in 1914, when she was in her mid-thirties.

Their life as a family came crashing down in 1915. Harry was shot and killed in his office by J. N. Whisenhunt, a distraught man whom Harry helped indict in a bankruptcy case.

It all started with the demise of the Buford Dry Goods Store, a retailer in downtown Fort Worth in the process of bankruptcy. Harry was a trustee of the company, holding all documents and some of the money to pay the creditors until the case was resolved. What really bugged Whisenhunt was the criminal charges filed against him. One of the store's owners, T. J. Brock, and Whisenhunt, a manager, allegedly forged the books to make it look like the business was in good financial shape in order to buy more goods. Then they never paid for those goods.

Creditors moved in, and Harry was possibly a court mandated trustee to take care of the company's books and assets. As such, Harry testified before a grand jury the state of affairs as he saw them. The next day, Whisenhunt appeared at Harry's office. Not only was Whisenhunt in trouble from mismanaging the store, he had lost a great deal of money from a previously failed business.

Whisenhunt left his home in Dallas early on the day before Thanksgiving without telling his wife or son where he was going. He arrived at Harry's office around 9 o'clock and walked straight to Harry's desk. Harry rose from his desk but didn't get a chance to speak.

"You've done me dirt!" Whisenhunt said and fired the .45 caliber pistol in his hand.

Mary Melton, ironically another Melton in the Ledgerwood's story, was his secretary and the sole witness. She began running at the first shot, only to hear two more.

Drawn by the sound of gunshots or Mary's screams, a man came in. Harry was dead and Whisenhunt almost dead from a gunshot to the chest. Not only did Whisenhunt have the .45, he also had a small automatic in his pocket.

Two wives became widows that day.

Ella was now a single parent with a daughter to raise. She returned to teaching, this time in Fort Worth high schools, eventually earning a Master's from Texas Christian University in 1933. She continued to exhibit her work in art shows about once a year and influenced local artists.

In the 1940 census, she owned a house on Hemphill Street and all her family lived with her with except her daughter, Alice. She'd married and moved to Houston. Ella's father outlived her by about a year.

Ella
Ray
Ledgerwood

*Courtesy,
Texas Wesleyan University
Special Collections.*

Paintings by
Ella Ray
Ledgerwood

*Courtesy,
Randy Tibbits and
Morris Matson.*

TWENTY-SEVEN
POLY SPORTS

Sports? Or no sports? How can a college not have sports? With administrators just trying to keep the school afloat, sports were low on the list of priorities. Even though all students were encouraged, really expected, to get some physical exercise, there was no room at first for team sports. Indeed, the *Fort Worth Gazette* reported that the Fort Worth Panthers, a semi-pro baseball team that organized in 1888, was playing against a team from Polytechnic, J. W. Adkisson was quick to have a correction printed. No Polytechnic baseball on *his* watch!

In describing Polytechnic's early days, C. L. Browning said there were baseball and football teams as early as the first year, but he did not recall any inter-collegiate games. Leon Sensabaugh remembers teams forming in 1893 and a field day. Pick-up games seemed to be the extent of team sports for the first several years.

John Creed remembered "little or no intercollegiate meets of any kind" and suggested that all the competitive spirit went into the literary societies. He claims the whole school attended one of these events in Tehuacana for a debate contest between Trinity University and Polytechnic. The rivalry was not aimed just at opposing schools. At times their ire could be directed toward classmates in on-campus literary competitions. By this time there were two organizations for the men and two for the women, and society loyalty could lead to heated emotional outbursts.

The later part of the decade was described as having facilities provided for baseball, football, and basketball, but the policy of no sports competitions remained in place despite a picture taken of the baseball team in 1898. Apparently the students were not happy about the policy, either.

The lack of sports might have played a role in the inability to retain the Crutchfield siblings at Polytechnic. From 1892 to 1894, the Crutchfield kids were everywhere from music classes to elocution. Yet all of them would go on to graduate from Vanderbilt. Wallace Crutchfield in particular made a name for himself playing football.

He was a natural, standing 6' 4" and weighing 230 pounds. He played guard for the Vanderbilt Commodores. As guard, he was picked as an All-Southerner in 1899. If he played flag football with the Polytech boys, it must have been quite one-sided. Vanderbilt led the South in organizing collegiate athletics, forming the Southern Intercollegiate Athletic Association in 1894. One news account gushed that Wallace was known as "the biggest man that ever played on the Vanderbilt football team," at least for his day. He also broke the Southern record for shot-put and was well known for other track and field events.

Fast forward fifteen years: Wallace had become a pastor of renown as well as president of San Angelo Collegiate Institute where he took a turn coaching the football team. Unfortunately the team rarely won a game. He had more luck recruiting faculty, assembling a well-respected group. In 1915, a newspaper article reported he was now 320 pounds and "by sheer physical power could easily pull down the pillars of a temple of no mean size. But, unlike Samson, he has no such designs on the Philistines." Even with this impressive size, "it is said he can sprint over a 100-yard course in less than twelve seconds."

Polytechnic's loss was Vanderbilt's gain.

Vanderbilt Commodores 1899
Wallace Crutchfield seated second from the right.
Public Domain.

Polytechnic Baseball Team
1898

Bottom Row (left to right)
L.M. Heizer, ?, W.H. Shumate, Sam Oglesby, D.M. Cavaness
Middle Row:
Matthew Hilburn, Curtis Manor, C.A. Parsons, Sam Braswell
Seated:
Roy Estes, Sam Whitenberg, Pat Conder
Courtesy, Southern Methodist University Archives.

Courtesy, Oklahoma HIstorical Society.

TWENTY-EIGHT
PROFILE: FRED NEWSOM

J. F. Newsom, or Fred, was a fixture during Polytechnic's first decade. He received a B.S. in 1894 and was an active Philosophian. At commencement exercise, he participated in the oration competition with his piece "For what are we living?" as well as sang a solo, "After Nine."

Fred bounced around as an educator, first teaching, then being a principal, even returning to Polytechnic as the administrator of the sub-freshman department.

In 1897, Fred got another degree at Polytechnic, this time an A.B. Then more bouncing around—he was in Ardmore for a time. In 1907, he ran for district clerk in Guymon, Oklahoma, and won. He seems to have had a good run as district clerk, ran a profitable farm growing grapes, and then he was appointed assistant county treasurer. Of course, when he resigned his position as district clerk, there seemed to be a little matter of a missing $2,000, which insulted newspaperman Warren Zimmerman.

In 1907, Zimmerman bought the *Guymon Herald* newspaper. He updated and improved the paper's facilities and acted as editor and reporter. Zimmerman had been raised in a sod house on the Kansas prairie and went to another Wesleyan, Kansas Wesleyan College, at Salina and began work in the newspaper business almost immediately.

Zimmerman seemed convinced Fred was a crook. News reports written by Zimmerman turned decidedly nasty in 1912 toward many city and county officials generally, and Fred in particular. With each month that went by, he grew angrier and angrier—and so did his rhetoric. Fred was eventually tried for the missing $2,000, and Zimmerman was right there with a blow by blow of the trial. When the case was dismissed, he railed about legal maneuvering by Fred's lawyer, insinuating Fred got off on a technicality. This could have cost Fred the election for postmaster and Zimmerman gloated about it. Every time some news worthy item came up related in any way to Fred, Zimmerman had to get in a dig.

So when Zimmerman published the following article, Fred had had enough.

"This paper believes like Joe Folk, the great and good Democrat of Missouri, that a grafter is neither a democrat nor a republican, but a thief and a scoundrel. They know, themselves, that they are guilty and don't dare to make a break. And, like the ballot box robbery which has been hushed up, they don't dare open the inside and what's more they never will. We sincerely hate to use up all this space, but feel our readers will feel with us that we are justified in doing so in nailing such an un-Godly lie circulated by J. F. Newsom, a man despised and hated by his neighbors from whom he's borrowed sums from $1.00 to $5.00 and never paid back, a political degenerate who sacrifices those who made him and who hasn't a close, personal friend in Guymon—a recognized nonentity in the place he came from in Eastern Oklahoma—as willful and malicious a liar—as conceited and unprincipled a rascal as ever followed the frontier to hide his sins."
—Warren Zimmerman.

Fred took Warren Zimmerman all the way to the Oklahoma Supreme Court for libel and slander. He could have brought a gun to the newspaper office and gotten Wild West justice, but he did the civilized thing and had his day in court. Zimmerman could not satisfy the court of any truth in his published account. The judgment was that Zimmerman had to pay $1,000 for damages.

Zimmerman never testified in his defense because "to set forth the answer would serve no useful purpose." Not sure what his answer would have been, but it sounded rather personal.

By the end of 1915, Fred retired from the life of a politician. He and his wife both became county agents in Beaver, Oklahoma, about seventy miles east of Guymon. They eventually resigned and left in 1919.

On the way out of Guymon, Zimmerman couldn't resist publishing one last parting shot along the lines of "good riddance."

Zimmerman left in 1915, not long after Fred. He sold the *Herald* and bought the *Liberal Kansas News*, returning to his home state and apparently never leaving again.

Fred eventually put his county agenting to good use and went to work for the railroad, helping them manage the land they owned.

Photo of Fred Newsom on previous page: Courtesy of Southern Methodist University Archives.

TWENTY-NINE

PROFILE: SAM KANOUSE

Many sets of siblings and cousins attended Polytechnic. The school fostered a family atmosphere and with its free tuition for preachers' kids, there were many families who took advantage of that. Sam and Anna were not preachers' kids. Their father was a businessman in Bowie and wanted his children to get an education.

Sam received his commerce degree in 1895. While in college, he focused his efforts on such business classes as bookkeeping and typewriting. He made time for other things: he took elocution classes and appeared to be a Philosophian in good standing. He was vice-president of the Epworth League, showing initiative to support the church's programs.

Surprisingly he could sing well enough without lessons that he did a duet with Lizzie Adkisson titled "A. B. C." for the Philosophian part of the commencement exercises in 1894. On the same program, he recited a work called "Was So Far Away." All these show a young man taking advantage of all the college had to offer.

Sam went to work for the railroad, probably the Rock Island Line in Fort Worth. According to family records, he worked his way up the company ladder, listing some of the jobs he had at the railroad yard.

Looking at job descriptions from NEGenWeb, the life of a railroad worker was rigorous and physical until he rose to management positions. By the time Sam worked in the railroad yard, locomotives were far safer than even ten years earlier thanks to inventions and innovations. He worked as a fireman, shoveling coal in the engine's firebox to keep the temperature high. Even in the train yard, locomotives needed thrust to move around. Switch-engine firemen worked only in the yard while road firemen traveled with the trains. The next job up was hostler.

The hostler would move the engine to the roundhouse. From there, he could move up to a switch-engine engineer. He moved other cars around in the railroad yard, guiding loaded box cars to their assigned engine. Another job his family listed specifically was switchman who literally hooked cars together, sometimes even when the cars were moving. The newly invented automatic couplers made this job safer, but there was still the chance he could be crushed between cars.

Sam was an engine foreman, which meant he could have been responsible for getting the engines and cars in the proper order or that he worked with the fireman to make sure the boiler had enough water and the fire was high enough. Sam definitely worked his way up to yardmaster, gaining that much more responsibility.

Dollie Wright was the daughter of another businessman from Bowie. Their fathers may have known each other. She forged a career for herself by getting a diploma from Fort Worth Business College. Dollie worked as secretary for a cattle company, eventually gaining the title Executive Secretary for grain companies that operated out of Fort Worth and Kansas City.

Sam and Dollie married in 1909. Dollie was thirty-two, Sam was thirty-three. They moved to Amarillo where, in all likelihood, Sam went to work for the Sante Fe Railroad. And nine months to the day, their one and only child, Edgar Laroe, was born.

Sam and Dollie Kanouse Wedding Day Portrait
November 24, 1909
Courtesy, Kent Kanouse.

James Albert Kanouse Family, c. 1900
Flora and James (lower right) with their grown children Anna and Sam (upper right). Anna's husband Noble Adkisson is at upper left; Charles and Anna's children Albert and Ruth are at lower left.
Courtesy, Kent Kanouse.

THIRTY
EVERYTHING THAT COULD GO WRONG AND DID

Every year, Polytechnic's student enrollment increased. Yet under the surface, things were not going well. In fact, the college was in a life and death struggle. What began with tremendous optimism (a college of many arts!) quickly faced harsh reality. Keeping this college going would not be easy.

Still operating with limited funds, Polytechnic opened their second school year, 1892-93, with the same buildings they started with. The school opened a small library with 551 mostly donated books. Half way through the school year, the U. S. economy began to fray. By March, the country was in a full-on financial depression.

Effects of the Panic of 1893 included:
- Value of the dollar was sixty cents and dropping.
- Livestock sold at such a low price it cost more to feed them than could be made selling them.
- Cotton dropped to less than eight cents a pound.
- Banks were forced to close.
- Businesses failed.
- Railroads were hit so hard construction came to a halt.

How were students impacted by these conditions? No doubt some of them could no longer afford college, especially those young men who had to work to contribute to the family's finances. The college still needed income but where would it come from?

J. W. Adkisson may not have had any fight left in him, since he resigned and said he wanted to go back to preaching. When Reverend W. F. Lloyd took over he had a mess, but he also had a bigger network of local businessmen because he had been the pastor at First Methodist Church of Fort Worth. Not only did businessmen weather the panic better than farmers and ranchers, they had expertise that could help guide the reverend.

Because his father died when he was nine, W. F. had to go to work to help his family's finances. He was licensed to preach at age eighteen. When he was assigned to the South Georgia conference, he became friends with Bishop Key. Through that connection, William found himself in Fort Worth. Mainly self-taught and trained in the school of hard knocks, he had a special blend of expertise to lead a struggling school.

Reverend W. F.'s church offered to continue paying him a salary so the college would not have to. In turn, he invested his own money for faculty salaries and repairs to the buildings. The college sold those lots on credit in Polytechnic Heights, then borrowed against the notes to run the school. In the Panic, the bank foreclosed on all of it and the land was lost. The college was forced to return to their donors time and time again.

Polytechnic just could not seem to get a break, but they kept limping along. Reverend Lloyd and the trustees never gave up. They made what improvements they could to the campus with plants and gravel walkways and continued to hold class.

Then there were the naysayers who grumbled about Polytechnic. Some in the Methodist conference thought that Polytechnic's very existence threatened the other Methodist college in the state: Southwestern in Georgetown. The funds from the conference were split between the two colleges, and the potential student base was also split, which they claimed weakened both. The Panic of 1893 made folks especially touchy about money. Yet Polytechnic kept attracting students in spite of or because of their business degree plans.

There was a near breaking point in 1899. Not because of money or disfavor, but because of some nasty diseases.

The year started pleasantly enough, but as the school year was winding down to the end of the spring semester, waves of epidemics moved across Texas. Outbreaks of measles, meningitis, flu, and pneumonia took over.

When a case of smallpox showed up at Polytechnic College on April 30, 1899, Reverend William must have felt he had no choice. He closed the campus for that school year and sent everyone home. He knew it would cause a financial burden and a devastating lack of faith, but he had to do it for the health of the entire student body, now around 400. The paper quoted Dr. Lloyd as saying "on account of this unfortunate affair the college will sustain a loss of not less than $40,000."

Years later, former trustee R. C. Armstrong said that bankruptcy had been almost a sure thing. Closing the school because of health concerns saved the school from bankruptcy.

W. F. was a man of God. He cared about the students, but he was also desperate to keep this college going. For a man who had little formal education, he must have wanted to leave his mark with a college but it was too much. He resigned and transferred to another conference. His friend would later write, "For five years under the most unfavorable conditions he strove as heroically and unselfishly to establish a first-class college for the church as it was possible for a man to do so. But while he failed to accomplish fully his cherished ideal, he made it possible for successors under more favorable conditions, to build up a great school which is largely indebted to Dr. Lloyd for the foundation laid."

Panic of 1893
Public Domain.

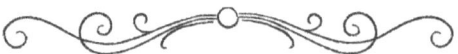

Anton Laporte Thomas

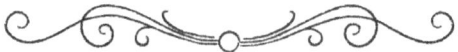

EVERY FAMILY · SCHOOL · LIBRARY STUDENT · · · · PERSON WHO READS OR WRITES
SHOULD OWN A DICTIONARY.

Care should be taken to GET THE BEST.

Webster's International, new from cover to cover, is the one to buy.

It is a thorough revision of the authentic "Unabridged," fully abreast of the times. The work of revision occupied over ten years, more than a hundred editors being employed and over $300,000 expended.

SOLD BY ALL BOOKSELLERS.

G. & C. MERRIAM CO., Publishers,
Springfield, Mass., U. S. A.

☞ Do not buy reprints of obsolete editions.
☞ Send for free pamphlet containing specimen pages, illustrations, and full particulars.

WEBSTER'S INTERNATIONAL DICTIONARY

Photo of Anton Laporte Thomas courtesy of Amy Ahlbrand Robinson, M. Ed.

THIRTY-ONE

PROFILE: ANTON LAPORTE THOMAS

Anton Laporte Thomas's great-granddaughter Amy remembers him as kind and patient, never saying a bad thing about anyone. Was he always this way or had he mellowed in his years serving Ennis as their doctor? After all, doctors see everything.

While at Polytechnic, Anton did not divide his attention with music lessons but stayed focused on his science studies. He graduated in 1900 and proceeded to Washington University to get his medical degree.

Perhaps there is something about being a doctor that makes a man go slow and steady. At seventy-eight years old, he won the Texas Medical Association's award for "General Practitioner of the Year." The year before, he won "Outstanding Citizen of Ennis." It was estimated that Anton delivered around 3,000 babies.

The day the TV news folks from Fort Worth came to interview him, one of those babies, now a boisterous ten-year-old, was in his office bleeding from a head wound, apparently the victim of a schoolyard collision with a baseball bat. Anton patched him up and sent him on his way while saying he was surprised to be named Practitioner of the Year.

He and his wife Edna Mae went to the Methodist church, even donating the land the building sat on. He was a Mason and a Shriner. When Anton and Edna Mae took a trip to the Holy Land, he showed slides at the Christian church.

So Amy was dumbstruck when the family revealed that her great-grandfather called a woman "as mean as a snake."

However, the woman in question birthed Clyde Barrow of the outlaw team Bonnie and Clyde. The thing Anton mentioned in passing was that he never got paid for any of Mrs. Barrow's births (she had three of them). His (slight) irritation revealed that he did occasionally lose his temper and was opinionated.

Maybe his nature was just that laid back, but he took care of everyone in his little part of the world. Rich or poor, getting paid with chickens or vegetables, he still took care of them. In fact, he continued to show up for work until age ninety-three.

THIRTY-TWO
CLASS OF 1900

What an amazing picture!

The Polytechnic graduating class of 1900. Most of the young men and women are identified but let's see what we can make of these outstanding young people.

Photo courtesy of Amy Ahlbrand Robinson, M. Ed.

The first man standing on the left is Stuart Lloyd. He was the son of W. F. Lloyd, the president of Polytechnic. He earned his A.B. at Polytechnic and M.A. at University of Texas. His fifty-year career in education was spent in Grapevine, Plano, Garland, and Austin but most of the time was spent in Dallas. He married Lizzie Chandler in 1900 and they had two sons.

Next to Stuart is Charles Owen, who earned an A.B. He went to Tennessee for a while then ended up in the Dakota Territory. He worked as a realtor and a "locator," someone who would find land for people who wanted to homestead. He was called "Owen, the Map Man." He met Anna Kositzky and settled down in the Dakotas.

The man in the picture next to Charles is unidentified, but there is one additional name on the graduate list. By process of elimination, the unknown person in the picture could be John W. Bagby. John settled in Edna, Texas, as a realtor and insurance salesman and served two terms as county judge. He married Minnie Pettway Tribble and they had one daughter.

Next to Charles is J. J. Creed. He was a very active member of the Polytechnic alumni, and was well acquainted with many students since he entered the college in 1892. J. J. was licensed to preach in 1898 and graduated with a B.L. in 1900. He became a pastor of renown throughout north and central Texas. He married Nola Brown after graduation and they had eight children.

Next to J. J. is Forest Uhl. Even though he earned an A.B., he went on to a career as a civil engineer after studying at Vanderbilt. He was the Superintendent of County Roads for Dallas County but would later relocate to Manhattan as a civil engineer for the city of New York.

Last on the standing row is Charles Morton, who earned a B.L. He went directly into the ministry upon graduation and was transferred to the Houston district. There he met and married the captivating Bessie Warner. In a review of one of her performances, a reader admired "her rich, full, exquisite, sweet contralto," which must have helped out in the many church choirs Charles served over his career. When he retired from active ministry, they settled into Mexia and continued to serve, finally relocating to Big Spring where he "mastered the art of visiting the sick and the shut-ins." Charles and Bessie had five daughters.

The first man seated at the left is Antone Laporte Thomas. From Polytechnic he went to Washington University for his medical degree and settled in Ennis in 1904. He would practice medicine until his death at ninety-three, always wanting to show up because people needed him. In 1953, he was named outstanding citizen of Ennis, then in 1954, the Texas Medical Association named him "General Practitioner of the Year." He married

Edna Mae Williams in 1906 and they helped Ennis grow to the community it is. They had four daughters.

Next to him are two unidentified women. There are two possibilities: Annie Owen and Nola Brown. Annie was sister to Charles, the man who would relocate to the Dakotas. She would marry a man in Tennessee and have a bunch of kids. The woman next to Anton seems to resemble the man behind her, so the guess is she is Annie.

That would leave the woman in the middle as Nola Brown, and she is seated in front of her future husband, J. J. Creed. Known as "Miss Nola," she showed leadership in all the college and local church activities. A friend would later gush, "My own life has been enriched by having known this dear Christian woman."

The last seated woman is identified as Nannie Lou Grace and beside her is her future husband, Tom Davis. They would go on to be a power couple in Denton, where he would serve as City Attorney for many years. They had three children.

Congratulations, class of 19-aught-aught.

Fifty Years Later ...
1941

Stuart M. Lloyd and
Lizzie Chandler Lloyd
of Dallas, Texas.

Charles Noble Adkisson
(left) and
Reverend
Frank P. Culver, Sr.

Clement A. Boaz (left) and
Dr. Leon F. Sensabaugh,
superintendent of
religious education at
Southern Methodist University.

Photographs on this page: Courtesy, Fort Worth Star-Telegram Collection, Special Collections, The University of Texas at Arlington Libraries.

CONCLUSION

Ten years had passed. Fort Worth still had a bit of an identity crisis with cowboys mingling with bankers and real estate men. The ladies finally got their library in 1901, thanks to a grant from Andrew Carnegie. Packing houses brought a boom of business in 1902. Quiet residential neighborhoods flourished with stately houses bought by big money. One of the tallest buildings in the city, the Wheat Building, put an elegant garden restaurant on the roof. Carriages drawn by horses would give way to electric streetcars. In spite of all the economic growth, or maybe because of it, saloons still did a brisk business.

There were ups and downs at Polytechnic as well, of course. With the turn of the century, a sense of optimism returned. Dr. Lloyd was worn out and resigned in 1899 after the bankruptcy scare and the disease outbreaks. Professor B. B. McSwain served as interim president for one year. When G. J. Nunn came on board in 1900, with his Vanderbilt credentials in tow, he started a building campaign that saw at least a new brick women's dormitory.

Enrollment had steadily increased in its first decade. That was not the problem. As always, the problem was money. To keep the cost down for students, the board fees barely covered the students' living expenses. Tuition could not pay the faculty's salary. The buildings had to be maintained, never mind building new ones.

Someone during the decade put in work on the grounds. With the emphasis on student participation, it may have been their efforts that transformed hard prairie into an attractive campus. Gravel walks and planted trees made the campus feel like a home, along with laughing voices and ardent efforts of students happy with their life at Polytechnic. There were areas set aside for games such as baseball and football, even if there were no formally organized teams.

Money had to come from somewhere, and Nunn did not seem to do much about the debt he was incurring. The optimism would not last. Nunn only lasted a year before Polytechnic found their new bold leader, Hiram Boaz, cousin to one of Fort Worth's city leaders, W. J. Boaz. Hiram would later write about how he was not sure he could save Polytechnic because of the overwhelming debt.

That is another story.

For now, Polytechnic would put one foot in front of the other, educate the students before them whether they were musicians, ministers, or bookkeepers.

They had the vision of being a civilizing presence on the prairie, creating not only leaders but leaders of character.

President Theodore Roosevelt plants a tree provided by Baker Brothers Nurseries at the downtown Carnegie Library in Fort Worth, 1905.
Courtesy, Library of Congress.

Presidents
Polytechnic College:
The First Decade

J. W. Adkisson
1891-1893

W. F. Lloyd
1893-1899

R. B. McSwain
1899-1900

G. J. Nunn
1900-1902

Acknowledgements

Writing a book with this many historical details can be daunting, especially when there was no student newspaper or yearbook. Relying on old newspapers and genealogical resources, I depended on archivists and historians more experienced than I.

Special thanks goes to Louis Sherwood, university archivist at Texas Wesleyan University, who always helped me track down the odd bit, the special picture, the "lost" information to enrich the story.

Other archivists include Jean Traster, Joan Gosnell, Elias Carreon, Sheila Bickle and Sarah Allsup.

Since this research was so much like genealogy, I also got a lot of help from family members such as John Tandy, Gene Leon Leonard, Amy Ahlbrand Robinson, and Kent Kanouse.

My coworkers have been very supportive of me: Dennis Miles, Marquel Anteola, Nancy Edge, and Elizabeth Howard. They let me try out most of the material on them before putting anything in the book. Thanks also goes to Michelle Hartman for her eagle-eyed copy editing and her always supportive friendship.

It is my great pleasure to thank Laurie Cockerell at Alliance for her superb orchestration of all the moving parts as well as Perry Cockerell for urging me to do the project in the first place.

Finally, Thea, Ethan and Aaron. Love you guys! You always have my back.

ENDNOTES

Chapter One
1 "Death of Mrs. J. W. Adkisson." Knox County Democrat, April 28, 1892.
2 *Rambler*, Oct. 29, 1997. https://texashistory.unt.edu/ark:/67531/metapth287694m1/4/?q=ghost+at+texas+wesleyan

Chapter Two
1 *Polytechnic College Catalogue* 1895, Chapter, 2, p. 8.

Chapter Five
1 Matthews, p. 54
2 https://texashistory.unt.edu/ark:/67531/metapth570441/m1/6/zoom/?q=%22w%20f%20mister%22&resolution=2&lat=2837.999999999998&lon=2773.5000000000014

Chapter Six
1 HeritageBattleCreek.org

Chapter Eight
1 https://socialwelfare.library.vcu.edu/woman-suffrage/women-in-nineteenth-century-america-2/

Chapter Fifteen
1 *Lampasas Leader*, July 20, 1934. https://texashistory.unt.edu/ark:/67531/metapth891779/m1/7/?q=murder+wife+dallas

Chapter Seventeen
1 https://www.brainpickings.org/2012/08/17/goethe-theory-of-colours/
2 *Panther City Parrot Yearbook*, 1906

BIBLIOGRAPHY

Alexander, Elizabeth, Brenda Matthews, and Louis Sherwood. *Texas Wesleyan University: the College on the Hill: 125 years of tradition, 1890-2015.* Franklin, Tn.: Grandin Hood, 2015.

Allen, Linda Gail. "Texas Wesleyan's Changing Dormitory Rules for Girls." Master's thesis, Texas Wesleyan, 1991.

"At What Point in History Did the Number 13 Become an Unlucky Number?" https://www.quora.com/At-what-point-in-history-did-the-number-13-become-an-unlucky-number

Boaz, Hiram. *Eighty-four Golden Years.* Nashville: The Parthenon Press, 1951.

Byerly, Victoria. *Hard Times Cotton Mill Girls.* Ithica: ILR Press, 1986.

Chapin, Charles V. "Variation in Type of Infectious Disease as Shown by the History of Smallpox in the United States 1895-1912." Journal of Infectious Diseases, V. 13, #2 (Sept. 1913), pp. 171-196. www.jstor.org/stable/30073361?seq=1#metadata_info_tab_contents

City of Fort Worth website: https://fortworthtexas.gov/

"Clarence Elbert Moore Manuscript 1975." Ruby Schmidt Collection of BiCentennial Interviews/Oral Histories of Fort Worth, Inc.

"Country Doctor and Bonnie and Clyde." Amy Ahlbrand Robinson, M.Ed. https://www.youtube.com/watch?v=bR7ch1JHI0Q

Cox, John Elmer. *A Brief History of Texas Wesleyan College.* Greeley, CO: Colorado State College of Education, 1953.

Deane, Edmund. *Branches of the Living Vine 1916-1991: A Seventy-five Year History of Highland Park United Methodist Church.* http://www.hpumc.org/archives/

Dent, Jim. *Twelve Mighty Orphans.* New York: St. Martin, 2008.

Family Group Sheet: Kanouse/Leath. Genealogy.com. https://www.genealogy.com/ftm/k/a/n/Kent-L-Kanouse/FILE/0002page.html

Find a Grave website: https://www.findagrave.com/

Friends of Tandy Hills website: https://www.tandyhills.org/

Fugate, Monette. *Polytechnic United Methodist Church, 1892-1992: a history.* Fort Worth: Polytechnic United Methodist Church, 1992.

Fung, Jason. "The Lucrative Story of Cotton Seed Oil." Diet Doctor website: https://www.dietdoctor.com/the-lucrative-story-of-cotton-seed-oil

Gateway to Oklahoma History. https://gateway.okhistory.org/

General Commission on Archives and History. Annual Conference Journal Memoirs Index. https://catalog.gcah.org:8443/exist/memoirs/memoirs.xql?show-form=yes

Haase, Daniel J. *Gateway to the West: A Historical Look at the Development of East Fort Worth and Its Neighborhoods.* Unpublished booklet, n.d.

Handbook of Texas website. Texas State Historical Association. https://tshaonline.org/handbook

Hemingway, Drenda. *The History of Literary Societies of Texas Wesleyan College.* Thesis, Texas Wesleyan, 1991.

Hometown by Handlebar. Mike Nichols blog about Fort Worth history. https://hometownbyhandlebar.com/

Johnson, Frank W. *History of North and West Texas.*

Johnson, Frank W. *History of Texas and Texans,* V. 3. Chicago: American Historical Society, 1916. https://books.google.com/books?id=LZNJAAAAYAAJ&pg=PA1218&lpg=PA1218&dq=%22fannie+tandy%22&source=bl&ots=r6uA3w87-6&sig=ACfU3U3XIK9nw2p8iFOa-csUz5vIPuNU6Q&hl=en&sa=X&ved=2ahUKEwiM9r3b9PLmAhVBIKwKHSreCIUQ6AEwAnoECAoQAQ#v=onepage&q=%22fannie%20tandy%22&f=false

Johnston, Richard. Interview

Kennedy, Oliver S. "Oliver S. Kennedy Papers." https://legacy.lib.utexas.edu/taro/utarl/02162/02162-P.html

Kilgore, Deborah Katheryn. "Interweaving History: The Texas Textile Mill and McKinney, Texas, 1903-1968." https://digital.library.unt.edu/ark:/67531/metadc12138/m1/1/

Knight, Oliver. *Fort Worth: Outpost on the Trinity.* Fort Worth, Tx: Texas Christian University Press, 1990.

Knott, Laura, Jeffrey Chusid and the University of Texas School of Architecture Historic Preservatin Program. "Cultural Landscape Report for The Browning Ranch, Blanco County, Texas." https://www.clbrowningranch.org/_images/pdf/collaborations.culture.pdf1.pdf

Matthews, Ben A. *A History of Polytechnic College.* Dallas, Tx: Southern Methodist University, 1930.

Mayo Clinic. "Smallpox." Mayo Clinic website: https://www.mayoclinic.org/diseases-conditions/smallpox/symptoms-causes/syc-20353027

McCarthy, Kayla. "A Day in the Life of a 19th Century IU Student." https://pride.iu.edu/pride-and-tradition/iu-history/19th-century-iu-student/

McMahon, Mary. "What is an Amanuensis?" WiseGeek.com. https://www.wisegeek.com/what-is-an-amanuensis.htm

Mitchell, Paul D. A History of the Methodist Church in Oklahoma. https://archive.org/stream/fromtepeestotowe01mitc/fromtepeestotowe01mitc_djvu.txt

Nichols, Mike. *Lost Fort Worth.* History Press, 2016.

Poly Alumni Association. History of Polytechnic. http://www.polyalumni.org/history.htm

Polytechnic College Catalogues, 1891-1901.

Popova, Maria. "Goethe on the Psychology of Color and Emotion." Brain Pickings. https://www.brainpickings.org/2012/08/17/goethe-theory-of-colours/

Portal to Texas History: https://texashistory.unt.edu/

"Railroad Job Descriptions." NE GenWeb Project website. http://www.usgennet.org/usa/ne/topic/railroads/job.html

Seeley, I. L. *Manual of College Literary Studies with Statistical Table*. Kalamazoo: Chaplin Book Printers, 1871.

Traster, Jean H. Interview

United States Dept. of State Office of the Historian. "The Philippine-American War, 1899-1902." State Dept. website: https://history.state.gov/milestones/1899-1913/war

Warder, Graham. "Women in Nineteenth-Century America." Social Welfare History Project. https://socialwelfare.library.vcu.edu/woman-suffrage/women-in-nineteenth-century-america-2/

Weinberg, H. Barbara. "William Merrit Chase (1849-1916)." The Met website: https://www.metmuseum.org/toah/hd/chas/hd_chas.htm

"What Do Trustees Do?" https://www.tc.columbia.edu/articles/2009/march/what-do-trustees-do/

Whitten, David. "The Depression of 1893." Economic History Association website. https://eh.net/encyclopedia/the-depression-of-1893/

PHOTOGRAPHS AND IMAGES

Introduction
(p. 5) Tandy Hills Natural Area: Photo by and courtesy of Don Young, 2019. Friends of Tandy Hills Natural Area website, https://www.tandyhills.org/notes/pics-proverbs-2019. The area has not changed much from when the Methodists first staked their claim.
(p. 7) Wellge, H, and American Publishing Co. Perspective map of Fort Worth, Tex. [Milwaukee, American Publishing Co, 1891] Map. https://www.loc.gov/item/75696592/. Courtesy, Library of Congress, Geography and Maps Division.
(p. 8) Texas Spring Palace, Fort Worth, Texas. Photo by G.C. Rhine, June 1889. Courtesy, *Jack White Photograph Collection*, Special Collections, The University of Texas at Arlington Libraries.

Chapter 1
(p. 9) Earliest photo of Polytechnic campus, c. 1892. Courtesy of Texas Wesleyan University Special Collections (Maud Hunter Collection).
(p. 11) Photo of official painted presidential photograph of Rev. J.W. Adkisson. Courtesy of Texas Wesleyan University Special Collections.
(p. 12) Polytechnic Cemetary. Photograph by Risa Brown.

Chapter 2
(p. 15) [Photograph of Students Sitting in a Classroom], photograph, [1900..]; (https://texashistory.unt.edu/ark:/67531/metapth861209/: accessed January 21, 2020), University of North Texas Libraries, The Portal to Texas History, https://texashistory.unt.edu; crediting Salado Public Library.
(p. 16) Drawing of the chemistry lab at Polytechnic. Illustration in *Polytechnic Catalogue*, 1891. Courtesy of Texas Wesleyan University Special Collections.

Chapter 3
(p.18) Advantages of Polytechnic College sign. Courtesy of Texas Wesleyan University Special Collections

Chapter 4
(p. 19) Photograph of C.L. Browning. *The Panther, Yearbook of Polytechnic College*, 1911, p. 38. Courtesy of Texas Wesleyan University Special Collections.
(p. 20) By Unknown - Mule drawn streetcar, Public Domain, https://commons.wikimedia.org/w/index.php?curid=32272001

Chapter 5
(p. 22) Polytechnic Faculty 1898. Courtesy of Texas Wesleyan University Special Collections (Maud Hunter Collection).

Chapter 6
(p. 24) Battle Creek Sanitarium with tower addition, a postcard, sent on December 10, 1928. The Willard Library collection. The Willard Library - http://dspace.willard.lib.mi.us/xmlui/handle/123456789/9690?show=full. [Public Domain.]

(p. 25) T.L. "Lee" Rippey and wife Mamie, c. 1900. Courtesy Texas Wesleyan University Special Collections (Maud Hunter Collection).

Chapter 7

(p. 26) Men's Dormitory, also called Key Hall (named for Bishop Joseph Key), c. 1892. Courtesy of Texas Wesleyan University Special Collections (Maud Hunter Collection).

(p. 28) Lucie Kidd-Key Photograph, c. 1898. Courtesy Texas Wesleyan University Special Collections (Maud Hunter Collection).

Chapter 8

(p. 31) Women's dormitory room. Illustration in the *Polytechnic Catalogue*, 1895. Courtesy of Texas Wesleyan University Special Collections.

(p. 32) Swartz. Beall Sawyer with Classmates, photograph, Date Unknown; (https://texashistory.unt.edu/ark:/67531/metapth38695/: accessed January 15, 2020), University of North Texas Libraries, The Portal to Texas History, https://texashistory.unt.edu; crediting Private Collection of the Ellis and Blanton Families.

Chapter 10

(p. 34) Arch Hall Photograph. Centennial Album, P. 1. Courtesy of Texas Wesleyan University Special Collections.

(p. 37) W.D. Hall Photograph. Centennial Album, P. 1. Courtesy of Texas Wesleyan University Special Collections.

(p. 38) Photo by Star-Telegram photographer Wilburn Davis, from a series under the headline "Behind-the-Scenes Men Responsible for Masonic Home's Gridiron Success," 11/06/1941. Courtesy, *Fort Worth Star-Telegram* Collection, Special Collections, The University of Texas at Arlington Libraries.

(p. 39) Hall Family Photo; courtesy of family member Gene Leon Leonard, grandson of Eva, great-grandson of Arch; photograph c. 1920s.

Chapter 11

(p. 42) George Tandy Photograph. Centennial Album, P. 1. Courtesy of Texas Wesleyan Special Collections.

(p. 43) Tandy Lake Painting. Courtesy of the Tandy family.

Chapter 12

(p. 44) Berniece Leach Painting of Church, reproduced in *Polytechnic United Methodist Church, 1892-1992: a history*, p. 6. Courtesy of Texas Wesleyan University Special Collections.

Chapter 14

(p. 49) W.B. Forrest Home. By Renelibrary - Own work, CC BY-SA 3.0, https://commons.wikimedia.org/w/index.php?curid=20142549

Chapter 15

(p. 50) World War I Mess Line at Camp Bowie, Fort Worth, Tx. National Archives Identifier:45501068; Local Identifier:165-WW-278A-4 Creator(s):War Department.1789-9/18/1947 (Most Recent) From:File Unit: Military Administration - In Service of the Interior - Supply Service - Issuance of Rations in Camp, 1917 - 1918 Series: American Unofficial Collection of World War I Photographs,

1917 - 1918. Record Group 165: Records of the War Department General and Special Staffs, 1860 - 1952. https://catalog.archives.gov/id/45501068

Chapter 16

(p. 55) Dr. W.F. Lloyd and family, c. 1900. Courtesy of Texas Wesleyan Special Collections (Centennial Collection).

Chapter 17

(p. 56) Literary Societies Editorial Staff, 1901. Insert in *Polytechnician*, December 1901, opposite P. 9. Courtesy Texas Wesleyan University Special Collections.

(p. 58) Adkissonians Literary Society Photograph, 1901. Insert in *Polytechnician*, December 1901, opposite P. 16. Courtesy Texas Wesleyan University Special Collections.

(p. 59) Philosophians Literary Society Photograph, 1901. Insert in *Polytechnician*, December 1901, opposite P. 17. Courtesy Texas Wesleyan University Special Collections.

Chapter 18

(p. 62) Susan M. Key Literary Society Photograph, 1901. Insert in *Polytechnician*, December 1901, opposite P. 8. Courtesy Texas Wesleyan University Special Collections.

Chapter 19

(p. 68) Smallpox Sign; San Francisco, California; : Buckley & Curtin, [191-] - Courtesy of the National Library of Medicine. Images from the History of Medicine (IHM), http://ihm.nlm.nih.gov/images/A21137. Also showcased in the book: *Hidden Treasure* (New York, NY: Blast Books, 2012), p. 178. HMD Prints & Photos call number: WA 234 C25 no. 14 sol. https://commons.wikimedia.org/wiki/File:Smallpox_keep_out_of_this_house..JPG#/media/File:Smallpox_keep_out_of_this_house..JPG

Chapter 20

(p. 70) Hine, Lewis Wickes, photographer. Fourteen year old spinner in a Brazos Valley Cotton Mill at West. Violation of the law. Matty Lott runs six sides. See family group and their story. Location: West, Texas. Texas United States West, 1913. November. Photograph. https://www.loc.gov/item/2018677658/. Courtesy Library of Congress.

(p. 70) Grocery store. Courtesy of Texas Wesleyan University Special Collections (Dillow Collection).

(p. 73) Sanborn Fire Insurance Map from Fort Worth, Tarrant County, Texas. Sanborn Map Company, Feb, 1893. Map. https://www.loc.gov/item/sanborn08530_003/. Courtesy of Library of Congress.

(p. 73) Neighborhood Antique Street Map: 1000+ Lost Texas Maps. Public Domain. https://www.facebook.com/lamotx/

Chapter 21

(p. 74) Portraits of Noble and Anna Adkisson. Extracted from Kanouse Family Portrait, c. 1908. Courtesy Kent Kanouse.

(p. 76) Ad for Noble Adkisson's play. *Polytechnic Catalogue*, 1893, P. 47. Courtesy of Texas Wesleyan University Special Collections.

Chapter 22
(p. 78) Strawman Clip Art by johnny_automatic. Vector Me website; https://vector.me/browse/173808/straw_man_clip_art
(p. 79) Oratory Contestants, 1893. Insert in Polytechnician, May 1903, front piece. Courtesy Texas Wesleyan University Special Collections.
Chapter 23
(p. 80) By Unknown - Front cover of the first Crisco cookbook, published in 1912. This file was obtained from the crisco website in the timeline section [2]. This work is in the public domain in the US per Wikipedia:Public domain because it was published before 1923., Public Domain, https://commons.wikimedia.org/w/index.php?curid=1489289
(p. 81) Leon Sensabaugh portrait. Extracted from Graduating Class of 1898 photo. Courtesy of Southern Methodist University Archives.
(p. 83) Photo of Ludi Mae from article Dallas Historical Society. Legacies: A History Journal for Dallas and North Central Texas, Volume 16, Number 2, Fall, 2004, periodical, 2004; from the collections of the Dallas History and Archives Division, Dallas Public Library.
(p. 84) Graduating Class of 1898. Courtesy of Southern Methodist University Archives.
Chapter 24
(p. 86) 1899 US troops in action during Philippine-American War. Original caption is 'Our Boys entrenched against the Filipinos.' Public Domain, https://commons.wikimedia.org/w/index.php?curid=2163058
Chapter 26
(p. 95) Ella Ray Ledgerwood Photograph. *Panther City Parrot: Yearbook of Polytechnic College*, 1906, p. 22. Courtesy of Texas Wesleyan University Special Collections.
(p. 96) Photographs of paintings by Ella Ray Ledgerwood. Photos courtesy of Randy Tibbits and Morris Matson.
Chapter 27
(p. 98) Vanderbilt Commodores 1899; Wallace Crutchfield seated second from the right. Wikimedia Commons, accessed 1/19/2020, public domain https://commons.wikimedia.org/wiki/File:1899Vandy.jpg
(p. 99) Polytechnic Baseball Team. Courtesy of Southern Methodist University Archives.
Chapter 28
(p. 100) Zimmerman, Warren. The Guymon Herald. (Guymon, Okla.), Vol. 22, No. 31, Ed. 1 Thursday, October 10, 1912, newspaper, October 10, 1912; (https://gateway.okhistory.org/ark:/67531/metadc274366/: accessed January 29, 2020), The Gateway to Oklahoma History, https://gateway.okhistory.org; crediting Oklahoma Historical Society.
(transparency p. 100) Zimmerman, Warren. The Guymon Herald. (Guymon, Okla.), Vol. 20, No. 32, Ed. 1 Thursday, October 20, 1910, newspaper, October 20, 1910; (https://gateway.okhistory.org/ark:/67531/metadc272854/: accessed

January 30, 2020), The Gateway to Oklahoma History, https://gateway.okhistory.org; crediting Oklahoma Historical Society.

(p. 101) Fred Newsom portrait. Extracted from Graduating Class of 1898 photo.

Chapter 29

(p. 104) Sam and Dollie Kanouse Wedding Photo, c. 1909. Courtesy Kent Kanouse.

(p. 105) Kanouse Family Portrait, c. 1908. Courtesy Kent Kanouse.

Chapter 30

(p. 109) English: "The recent panic scene in the New York Stock Exchange on the morning of Friday, May 5th." Illus. in: Frank Leslie's Illustrated Newspaper, 1893 May 18, p. 322. https://commons.wikimedia.org/wiki/File:Panic_at_the_NYSE_5_May_1893_cph.3b13869.jpg [Public Domain]

Chapter 31

(p. 110) Anton Laporte Thomas portrait. Extracted from Graduating Class of 1899 photograph. Courtesy of Amy Ahlbrand Robinson, M.Ed.

Chapter 32

(p. 113) Polytechnic Graduating Class of 1900. Courtesy of Amy Ahlbrand Robinson, M.Ed.

Fifty Years Later

(p. 116) Homecoming attendees Mr. and Mrs. Stuart M. Lloyd, 5/24/1941; Courtesy, *Fort Worth Star-Telegram* Collection, Special Collections, The University of Texas at Arlington Libraries.

(p. 116) Charles Noble Adkisson (left) and Rev. Frank P. Culver at Texas Wesleyan commencement exercise; 5/26/1941. Courtesy, *Fort Worth Star-Telegram* Collection, Special Collections, The University of Texas at Arlington Libraries.

(p. 116) Two homecoming attendees Clement A. Boaz (left) and Dr. Leon F. Sensabaugh; 5/24/1941. Courtesy, *Fort Worth Star-Telegram* Collection, Special Collections, The University of Texas at Arlington Libraries.

(p. 118) Swartz, C. L, photographer. Pres. Roosevelt's visit, Fort Worth, Texas / photo by C.L. Swartz, 702 Houston St., Fort Worth, Texas. Fort Worth Texas, 1905. Apr. 8. Photograph. https://www.loc.gov/item/2013651329/.

Cover

Polytechnic Graduating Class of 1900. Courtesy of Amy Ahlbrand Robinson, M.Ed.

Shutterstock: Old Paper Texture by Lukasz Szwaj

*Various embellishments and old advertisements throughout the book can be found in *Polytechnic Catalogues*, c.1892-1899. Courtesy of Texas Wesleyan University Special Collections.

www.ingramcontent.com/pod-product-compliance
Lightning Source LLC
LaVergne TN
LVHW051600080426
835510LV00020B/3061